My Battle of Hastings

XIAOLU GUO

My Battle of Hastings

Chronicle of a Year by the Sea

Chatto & Windus
LONDON

3 5 7 9 10 8 6 4

Chatto & Windus, an imprint of Vintage, is part of the Penguin
Random House group of companies whose addresses can be
found at global.penguinrandomhouse.com

First published by Chatto & Windus in 2024

penguin.co.uk/vintage

Typeset in 10.6/14.5pt Minion Pro by Jouve (UK), Milton Keynes
Printed and bound in Great Britain by Clays Ltd, Elcograf S.p.A.

The authorised representative in the EEA is
Penguin Random House Ireland, Morrison Chambers,
32 Nassau Street, Dublin DO2 YH68

A CIP catalogue record for this book is available from the
British Library

ISBN 9781784745370

For Moon, a child who has come to know the ebb
and flow of the tides along the English Channel
and the sands without end on the coast of Normandy

The island Britain is 800 miles long, and 200 miles
broad. And there are in the island five nations; English,
Welsh (or British), Scottish, Pictish, and Latin.
The first inhabitants were the Britons, who came
from Armenia, and first peopled Britain southward.
Then happened it, that the Picts came south from Scythia,
with long ships, not many; and, landing first in the
northern part of Ireland, they told the Scots that
they must dwell there. But they would not give them leave;
for the Scots told them that they could not
all dwell there together.
ANGLO-SAXON CHRONICLE

Contents

AFTERWARDS

Battles produce corpses, multitudes of them. In a mass killing like the Battle of Hastings, almost a thousand years ago, hosts of living humans were transformed into corpses, bodies were strewn across mud and grass. Men believed in God then, and there must have been profound fears after the battle about what to do with these bodies. Mutilation of the victims was normal at that time. The rituals of treating the dead a thousand years ago are not entirely known to us, but certainly, if we have to, we can visualise shapeless body parts scattered over the fields. Hacked-off legs and arms, a chunk of flesh torn from the loins, the cleaved-open skull of a soldier, or disembodied guts above which dance a murder of crows with their dagger beaks. Some body parts might have been identified right after the massacre. For example, a half finger which might have belonged to King Harold, or an ear from one of Harold's brothers. All lifeless, bloody, smeared with the black soil of East Sussex. A layer of acidic earth enveloped those bones and those strips of skin, still slightly warm after being torn from their hosts. But soon these membranes, the soft and hard tissues, lost their integrity in the cold rain. Rats would have run around in ecstasy feasting on the fragmented flesh. Cats, foxes, weasels, boars, squirrels, worms, birds. Yes, birds, migrant birds or non-migrant ones. It must have taken some time for the birds to figure out how they should proceed with the human remains. Were they aware that there was no need for them to fight for their prey, at least not for some weeks or months?

In those days, some eagles were large and strong enough to grasp a child in their talons and fly off with it. One might find the body part of a foot soldier hundreds of miles away, in the north of England or the border around Wales, thanks to a large eagle. But wherever the corpses were, it must have taken years for them to completely decompose. Long after soft tissues had been leached away, skeletons or at least bones would remain, no longer recognisable as belonging to any individual. The wife could not find her husband in a pile of bones, nor the daughter her father. One cannot rule out that some feature in a whitened skull remained, allowing identification. The decomposition would depend on temperature, humidity, insects, animals around the bodies. And of course, water, and not just the English rain. Water would be a factor in deciding the pace of the decomposition, especially in the land along the English Channel. These moist lands are not like deserts where bodies can be preserved, or frozen wastes where a body can be dug up thousands of years later, still revealing its death agony.

On the battlefield, there would have been countless dead or injured horses, once well-trained Norman horses. They had made the horrible trip across the sea from Normandy, and survived the chaotic English landing, their solidly shod hooves cracking on the shingle beach, muzzles dragged and roped, their bulging eyes wet and glinting. I hear these animals crying in the thick of battle, stabbed by spears, hacked by axes, then collapsing under armour, or bolting riderless through fields, their flanks oozing blood. I see a grey stallion, a war saddle strapped on its back, its left foreleg bleeding, its hock damaged and its gaskins smashed. It runs but gradually slows down, then falls onto a broken branch by the edge of the fields. I search for the animal among the bushes. I see it again. Despite these wounds, its mane is totally intact.

After the battle, the Norman army was dispatched to other parts of England, and eventually marched towards London. William the Conqueror knew how to go forward on the back of success. Dead

Anglo-Saxons were left on the hills of East Sussex, or in time pushed into massive ditches by surviving locals. Yes, I imagine the locals would have had to do that, in order to avoid disease and plague. It must have been days after the battle, after rain and mist. The survivors, probably not many of them, mostly women and children, had to drag and push those bodies into mass graves. They must have been terrified doing this.

These days the field of the battle is serene and seemingly untouched by ancient agonies. It slopes gently down from the old abbey that was constructed on the top of the hill years after the slaughter. At the bottom of the hill are villages and farmlands that lead to the sea. There is a desolation here even though it is bathed in soft light and green hues. This desolation probably has little to do with its tortured history. When we find a place to be desolate, sad or abandoned, is it the place itself or us projecting our inner state? Or can we really separate the two?

Winter

Relocation

I am an immigrant. I am an artist and a woman. Being a woman does not entirely define me, being an artist describes more my way of living. It is true that I see myself as a writer and a film-maker first. I am old enough to say this, with a certain clarity in my mind. Since I left China, I have wanted to live life fully. I have wanted to explore, geographically and spiritually.

I became a British citizen some years ago, before Britain left the European Union. I had been living in London, in my partner's flat which he owns. I never had my own place, and I didn't mind. Having left China, I wasn't sure if I wanted to settle in England. This changed when my parents died of cancer, first my father, then a year later my mother. I gave birth to my own child during that time and briefly went back to China with my newborn baby. My brother and I managed to sell the family house where we grew up. All the memories associated with that house, occasionally joyful but mostly sad, seemed to evaporate in the sale. I would inherit half of the money, and when I returned to England, I thought, finally, I could have a place of my own. Once uprooted, now I could root myself again. But London had become so expensive, I could not afford to have my own place, not even a shed if I wanted to live in central London. All my life I wrote in my kitchen, because I never had my own workspace. Where could I find a room just to write, and to think by myself?

I thought about growing up by the East China Sea, and how we watched the waves every day on the littered beach. My grandfather was a fisherman, and spent all his life on his fishing boat, though none of us followed his path. My father loved the ocean, and painted seascapes all his adult life. I thought about the claustrophobic nature of London, and how much I missed the salty wind, the contour of shorelines, and the ceaseless changing waves in the viewfinder of my eyes. I decided to get a place by the sea, along the English Channel. I stopped visiting Europe and China. Instead, I put on my raincoat and wandered around by the English coast. Some days I went to Brighton and Southend, others I walked on the hills of Folkestone and Worthing, or rode buses around Margate, staring into the sand. And then I went back to Hastings. I still remember the first time I visited, right after I had left China. A friend of mine in London said she would take me to visit 'famous deaths in obscure locales'. This friend was a fan of the rock band INXS and the lead singer Michael Hutchence, who committed suicide in 1997. Though Hutchence did not die in Hastings, his lover Paula Yates, the TV presenter of *Big Breakfast*, had bought a seaside house in Hastings before their deaths. So there we were, wandering in the Old Town and looking up at a three-storey Georgian house where the rock star and his lover had fleetingly entwined their lives. It was an ordinary building with white walls and peeling paint. It was already owned by some other residents so we could not enter or see the garden in the back. Hutchence died by hanging himself and Yates died of an overdose. The impression of Hastings from that first visit was strange: a rain-stained dilapidated town with old people shuffling along on the pavement and a few homeless men hovering in street corners or sauntering by. During that trip I also learned that the occultist and magician Aleister Crowley had lived in Hastings for the last few years of his life and had died there. Back then I hadn't linked Hastings to the most famous battle of British history. An obscure place where the formerly celebrated went to die – that was my rather morbid understanding of the town. But curiously, that visit haunted me, as if it was a cursed place but, at the same time, sexy, mysterious and somehow quintessentially English. To my Chinese mind, in all its ignorance, Hastings seemed full of hauntological possibilities. The second visit to Hastings was more pleasant and positive: no rain or piercing wind. It was a sunny, blue-sky day as I walked along the coast towards Bexhill and Eastbourne. I did not think much of 'famous deaths in obscure locales' that time, all I thought about was a home by the sea.

I thought perhaps I could try to live in Hastings. So I went there and registered my details with an estate agent, followed by a string of viewings. Two weeks later, I called my brother in China to tell him I had found a place – in a town called Hastings. He had never heard of it. But he promised he would send me my half of the money from the sale of the family house.

The Residence

The first time I saw the impressive seafront premises in Hastings was in a brochure provided by my estate agent. It showed a five-storey building with an imposing Victorian facade. 'A stone's throw from Marina beach and walking distance to Hastings Castle,' said the advertisement, 'we are delighted to offer you this charming apartment with uninterrupted sea view.' The brochure showed the views and the interiors: a carpeted living room, a small bedroom, a narrow kitchen, and a miniature bathroom. Everything seemed to be modest, even a bit on the dingy side, but I did catch a glimpse of a white bathtub. I cannot live with just a sea view. A non-negotiable feature is a tub in which to soak my body in the endless cold English evenings. So sea view and tub, an indispensable pair, and a minimum if this acquisition is to do honour to the memory of my late parents.

I decided to see the legendary premises for real. On the day, ten minutes before the viewing appointment, I was told that the estate agent would be waiting for me at the site. But as I stood by the building, I could not find any door or bell number that corresponded to the address I had been given. I called the estate agent, but his phone was turned off. I looked around. I was indeed next to a grand court, the same facade as I saw in the brochure. But where to enter? And what were all these stores on the ground level? It seemed to be non-residential. On the left, Royal Carpeting

Hastings, with rows of carpets and rugs piled high in the window. Next to this, a Co-op supermarket with sea-themed toys for children – nets, boats, buckets, etc. – stacked on shelves from floor to ceiling. A large banner announcing a 10 per cent discount for seniors 'every Monday to Friday'. The elderly seemed to have a good deal here. On the right, a charity shop, a betting shop, and a take-away selling pizza and fries. Towards the end of the building a retail space entirely boarded up and covered in graffiti. But no entrance to this fine residential dwelling. I walked into the supermarket. The Indian man behind the counter was on his mobile. I stared at him and waited. A pensioner was picking up some discounted salad. Double discounted, in her case. Finally, the Indian man finished his phone conversation. I asked him where the residency entrance might be. He spoke with an accent I did not recognise: 'In the back,' he yelled. 'In the back!'

I walked round the building and found myself on a backstreet, the pavement littered with plastic bags, half-eaten bagels and pizza boxes. Between two parked trucks I saw an entrance. I pushed the heavy black door, so heavy I had to use both hands. I found myself in the hallway. A sudden ditch. I almost fell. I managed to steady myself and my eyes got used to the dark. I saw unopened letters scattered on the floor. I moved a bit, then a dim electric light sputtered on. I placed my foot on the blue carpet leading up the ornamental staircase to the flat I was about to visit. The sounds of two different television channels mingled and confused my senses. There I was, in a building from another century, trapped by time. I was on a spiral staircase, ascending, but somehow not quite getting to where I was supposed to go. Like an M. C. Escher drawing, I was caught in the loop of Moorish staircases. For an instant, I thought I was already in my future flat, while my body was still following the repetitive curves of the stairway. Just then, my phone rang. 'I'm so sorry, I'm running late ...' It was my estate agent, finally.

I received two sets of keys for the flat in December 2021. But I didn't have the courage to move in, not in this cold and wind. The weather had been so brutal. I hid in London at my partner's place with my child, cooking soup, keeping warm. I did not manage to write anything. At the beginning of the new year, just before the Russian invasion of Ukraine, when there was nothing much in the news apart from weary pandemic updates, I took out my keys and carried a heavy duvet and blankets into the Hastings flat.

The Consequences of War

The Consequences of War is the title of a painting by Peter Paul Rubens. When I first saw this painting I did not think for a moment that it referred to the Thirty Years War, which occurred within the Holy Roman Empire during Rubens' lifetime in the seventeenth century. With so many naked women, at a glance it more resembles an orgy than a scene of war. At its centre stands Mars, the god of war, in his shining helmet and red cloak. In his left hand he holds a shield, in his right he grips a sword that almost seems to protrude from his groin. He is casting a backward glance at Venus who, surrounded by Cupids, drapes her body around him in an effort to arrest his advance, as though the power of love might vanquish the will to destroy. Meanwhile the Fury Alekto urges him onward. His victims – men, women, children – lie prostrate at his feet. A woman dressed in a black robe raises her arms in despair, expressing, it seems, the distress of Europe.

Hastings is not Europe. But for me, it is. Because Hastings is the manifestation of the whole of Europe, and of the distress of Europe.

In my mind, Europe has always been at war. I am thinking not only about the First and the Second World Wars; it is a place that seems to have initiated most of the wars after the birth of Christianity. Returning to Rubens' time: the Thirty Years War, fought between Protestants and Catholics, involved nearly all the countries in central Europe. In the end, the Catholics won, and peace was temporarily restored, at a cost of 8 million people. Then there was the War of Spanish Succession at the beginning of the eighteenth century. Just for one clash during the Battle of Malplaquet, nearly 20,000 people died. Even more bloody wars followed in the nineteenth century, with millions perishing during the Napoleonic Wars. The Napoleonic Wars affected Britain so greatly that a large population of people were left in poverty and misery with high tax rates and unemployment. In my eyes, the Channel between France and England was a place of intensified conflict. And Hastings was the centre of that intensification, beginning with the famous battle from a thousand years ago. During my first visit to Hastings, as I was standing on a hill looking down to the English Channel after visiting the former houses of Paula Yates and Aleister Crowley, my friend said: 'So, here is where the Normans came and conquered England in 1066.' That day the waves in front of us were gentle, the wind light, just like the remote past which lies quietly buried under ferns spreading out beneath our feet. So ungraspable, so different from the angst and horror of Rubens' painting.

I have restarted my diary writing. It seems I have more time in Hastings. I began it in January 2022 and then in February a war broke out in Europe. Every day, morning and evening, newly updated images of the ongoing war have flooded the media wherever I go. Sometimes I am in a cafe, or on a train, or sitting at home,

where I am looking at the pictures: burned tanks, collapsed buildings, broken fences and machinery, as well as corpses lying around
in a destroyed Ukrainian town. Most of the time, I look at these
pictures in this very town called Hastings. The war that's happening
now in Europe makes me stare into history, just as I so often stare
into the waters of the Channel. Carried by the ceaseless coastal
wind whose temper I am beginning to get used to, I am being taken
back as far as a thousand years ago.

The Statues

I turn to the east, walking towards the beach in West St Leonards. A green meadow with trees and flower beds unfolds in the near distance. In that little park, I will meet two statues. I will visit the dying king, the last English king before the Norman Conquest, King Harold. A sad but powerful sight. Though he is not alone. A woman cradles his head in her arms, her face mournful, perhaps she is weeping. She is Edith Swanneck, Harold's first wife and perhaps the only woman he loved.

Neither figure of this double statue is standing. King Harold lies on his back, Edith Swanneck is on her knees. Suspended in motion, both are sorrowful and frozen in time. Their surfaces are breaking apart. Their white plaster skin is spotted with dirt and dust, their toes and hands are missing, as if they were suffering from a plague, or some horrible skin disease. The statues were made in 1875, by Charles Wilke. I haven't checked who this Mr Wilke was yet. The mournful sight of the statues always transports me back to the ancient past in an instant. With snowdrops and budding daffodils around my boots, lost in my thoughts, it feels like this place is suspended in a perpetual winter.

When I moved here, I knew only that the Battle of Hastings was fought between the French and the English. So, the terms 'French' and 'English' are shorthand for a complicated mix of Northern Europeans at that point. Perhaps it would take another lifetime for me to understand the DNA of those people – the fighters and the non-fighters, the islanders and non-islanders. The battle ended with the Norman French taking over Anglo-Saxon England, and with the slaughter of 10,000 men. What seems incredible is that the battle lasted only a day. Apparently King Harold was shot by an arrow in the eye – at least that's the most popular version of events in historical records. But whether it was an arrow that killed the king, or whether tens of thousands of men and women from these villages and farms died, what's all that to me? Me, a Chinese immigrant to Europe, a woman with neither power nor any Western ancestry, what is the connection? Nothing, not even in the most remote sense. Even my reimagining of that battle on the nettle-covered hills feels remote and distant. As I stand on the shingle beach of Hastings, I cannot see French land, or any island. It's all misty. It's beyond the white mist above the grey waves. There are only the loudly crying seagulls, the wind, and one or two sails in the distance.

A Foreigner

The past is a foreign country. This is true for me. But the past of Hastings and Anglo-Saxon history is doubly foreign.

For a non-Westerner like myself, to grasp the meaning of the word 'Anglo-Saxon' is as demanding as to understand the word 'Norman'. And to know what 'Norman' means, I have to be very patient, because I have to return to the age of Norse, the Vikings, the Celts, or to times and places even more remote than the remote culture where I am from. It's much easier for me to connect to the Mongols, the nomadic Asian people who conquered China in the thirteenth century. When I think of the Mongols I think of eagles, horses, Kublai Khan and ravaged cities. The gene pool of the Mongols is also where my people come from. But Norse and Vikings, those ice-capped lands and fur-covered people, would take me much longer to connect to. I shiver a little as though the temperature around me is dropping as my imagination travels. I picture animal skins and fur coats. Swords under sheepskin, snowflakes melting on eyebrows, scary sounds coming out from a foaming mouth. I may as well just read simple chronicles of the North instead of epic poetry – that might give me a better picture of history. Better is not the right word here. I know. But I cannot take any more prose. Especially sophisticated prose. Can't we get going, straight into history, without too much poetry along the way? Or too much of a narrative arc? I have been fed a succession of unreadable syllabi at university, in China as well as in Britain. Not quite unreadable, perhaps. But ungraspable, indigestible, incomprehensible. I am exhausted by elaborate narratives. I want direct knowledge. Why does acquiring knowledge have to be so complicated? I want to be connected to history directly, in a simple way. If I cannot, then I should just read myths. Hunters and crows, crying daughters and jealous fathers. Shipwrecks and the homecoming of heroes. How many myths can one read in one's life? Five hundred? Five thousand? The number of historical dramas we have watched and read in our lifetime is shockingly large, yet still people do not understand history. Though for some people, a very special kind of person, to know one myth (one myth entirely) is sufficient. Sufficient for what though? Sufficient to understand how our world is constructed. All they need is a copy of the Bible, or a translation of the Koran. Or a volume of the *Diamond Sutra*. But not all three. The illiterate just have to listen. But for the ones who can neither read nor listen, they just have to live in their dark world. Perhaps there are large numbers of people living in that dark world. I am one of them, I read only some parts of the *Diamond Sutra*, and I did it half-heartedly.

Here, under the hills of Sussex, or away from the beaches of Kent, if you go a little bit inland, you see people living in that dim dark world. Not entirely dark, but dark. Men and women are trapped in narrow Victorian houses, their heating switched off to avoid the gas bill. The locals or semi-locals drag themselves along the treeless streets, a shopping bag in hand. On a street corner littered with rubbish, a gaunt-looking man passes a little plastic sachet of drugs to another gaunt-looking man. Two youthful girls in tight dresses stroll past, giggling and chatting, a beer can in hand. The girls make me feel better, and gentler, even though God knows where they are heading after finishing their beers. And I can smell winter jasmine. Somewhere behind walls or fences, the jasmines are flowering and will bloom until spring arrives. I love winter jasmine. I love their star-shaped petals, yellow and white. They remind me of China and my childhood. There were always winter jasmines growing at the school campus and in every residential street. We would pick the flowers and decorate our hair before going to the cinema or attending a large family dinner. They also remind me that I have been banished, far from the world I come from. In China, if you look at the west of the globe, the end of the map is Britain, and that is how the Chinese visualise Britain in their mind's eye. But I cannot complain about being in Britain, since many people still try to get to this land regardless of its fading power. It is pathetic to complain. We are being blown into this world, like a jasmine seed in the wind. We drift and then we land somewhere, we try to grow in its soil. Winter comes, spring awaits. We either germinate or turn into dust.

Neighbours

I climb four flights. I still don't know any of my neighbours. Their doors are always closed. Of course, doors should be closed. Why would I think they should be different? An absurd notion. An open door is a by-product of the door's function. In my childhood province, doors were kept open, to reduce the humidity and heat. Only during the typhoon season would we shut the windows and doors against wind and rainstorms. But that was a different time and place. Now I climb up and up. There is a door on the left, and a second one on the right, and in between them a third. Every floor has three doors, except for my floor. I have never encountered anyone on the first floor. On the second floor, I have seen an Indian couple and an old lady with a dog. Both the lady and her dog have long grey hair. What kind of dog? Afghan hound? Pekinese? I am not a dog person. Neither the lady nor the dog seems to want to have a haircut. Now, as I climb, I can hear barking behind the closed door. I get to the third floor. I know that behind one of the closed doors lives a red-haired nurse in her sixties. I am not entirely sure she is a nurse, but the estate agent mentioned her to me, and indicated that she was the longest-standing resident in the premises. I have met this nurse a few times coming in and out. She has an unusual look. Her body language is slightly stiff, her face weary, her dyed red hair bunched tightly behind her head, revealing the grey behind her ears. Her hair does not look entirely like her own. She frowns and pulls herself back a little whenever she encounters me on the stairs or outside in the street. Is it just me she frowns upon? Or do other oddities suffer the same reception? I worry about how a newcomer like myself is perceived by the locals, although I wonder how local she really is. Perhaps she works for a care home and is poorly paid. Perhaps she is ill disposed towards the entire human race. Apart from this redhead, I know no one on the third floor. I have seen a few unfamiliar faces, strangers carrying suitcases up and down. Perhaps they are Airbnb guests? I get to the fourth floor where my flat is. The motion-sensitive light doesn't work, and I walk on the stairs in total darkness. There are only two flats on my level. And, as I fumble a bit in the pitch-black, I think to myself I should get to know my next-door neighbours a little. But I am not sure who really lives there. I have seen different people coming in and out. Once, a large canvas appeared, with a fresh odour of oil paint. The person carrying it was not instantly visible. I quickly scanned the painting: a red-brown female nude, deformed in an abstract way. But perhaps I was wrong. In the middle of her crotch there seemed to be what looked like a penis sticking out. The material used to construct this protuberance was either rubber or plaster. So, it was more than a painting, it was also a sculpture. The phrase 'her penis' came immediately to my mind. I had heard the phrase before, being discussed by newspaper commentators angry about trans issues. Then the person behind the canvas showed his face. He was a long-haired middle-aged man, unkempt with an artistic air. A casual hello was exchanged between us and I made a brief comment on the painting: 'That looks interesting, is it yours?' He answered 'yes', which was ambiguous for me. I did not understand if he was communicating that he was the painter of the work or that he owned it, or whether he meant that he had served as the model for the work of sculpture. Another time, I saw a Muslim woman in a grey hijab with a child following behind. We exchanged greetings before each of us closed our doors. And that has been the sum total of my interactions with my next-door neighbours.

Inside my flat, I make my way to the main window of the lounge and look at the sea. My favourite experience. As I take in the view, I think about my neighbours. I wonder about the connection between the artist and the Muslim mother. Did she approve of his painting? I wonder how these two very different occupants manage to cohabit. Then it strikes me how diverse the many inhabitants of this building are. I should not be surprised and I am not displeased. The world is always more varied and surprising than we think it is. I look again at the sea, and am soon distracted by several sails gliding above the waves.

Woman's Hour

I bring back a discount veg box this morning. It only cost £1.50, and consists of near-expired fruit and veg. The potatoes are a mouldy black, the grapes brown-green, the plums are squashed and stuck together. But the aubergine and carrots are perfectly all right. I can't complain. I am not a senior yet and I don't deserve a discount. In any case, supermarkets in Hastings seem to have a different pricing scale, even if the energy bills are just as high.

In my tiny kitchen I listen to the radio while sorting out the vegetables. The radio set is smaller than my kettle, and my kettle is only a little bigger than my cups. They work fine. It's a small flat and I am fortunately small too. While peeling leaves off the corn, I hear an interview on BBC Radio 4's *Woman's Hour*. 'A conscious sex worker' – that's what the interviewed person calls herself. 'Conscious' is the part that catches my attention. I turn up the volume. I have missed her name, but I understand that she works with disabled people. She talks about the sexual care of disabled people, particularly those who have suffered traumatic physical experiences. I stop picking out the rotten grapes from the box. 'I want my able body to help the disabled bodies.' Able body. Disabled body. How simply she expressed it. In any case she is a wonderful speaker, very eloquent. She goes on: 'I treat my sex work as a form of therapy for the disabled because sex plays such a key role for those people.' And: 'I can provide them sexual pleasure.' Her words are positive, spirited and dignified. At one point, the presenter questions her professional name. She calls herself 'Lady of the Night'. Yes, I am also unsure about that. What about being a lady of the *day*? It seems to be a lazy way of describing a very special service. 'Isn't it to define yourself as a prostitute, to call yourself Lady of the Night?' the presenter asks frankly. The sex worker neither denies nor affirms it. She takes it very lightly. She doesn't seem to care much about what she calls herself. Identity politics don't seem to apply to her, or political correctness. She then tells us that there is only one hotel in London that allows her to conduct her business, which requires special equipment. (I think I must have missed some key technicalities when she talked about bondage in her service.) I pick up a carrot and begin to peel it. I am amazed by how revolutionary her speech is, and how traditional my role is in the kitchen. What are the actual sexual acts she would have to adopt or invent when dealing with disabled bodies? Since it is on national radio, the presenter does not go into details. The programme ends with a comment from one of the listeners: 'What a fantastic speaker, this sex worker, a breath of fresh air!' – a tweet sent to Radio 4. I agree entirely. What a breath of fresh air. Even in old Britain. In fact, I must eradicate my prejudice, especially along the Channel, where fresh air is abundant.

Anglo-Saxon Chronicle

I am only at the beginning of my copy of the *Anglo-Saxon Chronicle* and am nowhere near the Battle of Hastings yet. Commissioned by Alfred the Great a thousand years ago, it is still a very interesting book to read. It is not quite a 'book', but an endless record of events, some maddeningly savage, others quite trivial. Before coming to Britain, I did not know such a chronicle existed. I lived in China most of my life. Back home I had to study similar chronicles, regardless of how tedious this was for a teenager who wanted to escape history. We had to memorise all the kings and their deeds during the Warring Dynasty or the names of the lords from the Song Dynasty. We had to write our lengthy homework under feeble light while our parents returned home late from their work. That was a long time ago. The *Anglo-Saxon Chronicle* is important, if you are interested at all in history. It gives us some vital facts about who did what when, but also gives us insight into how people then thought of their own history. The chroniclers were diligent and devoted monks who lived in cave-like monasteries. They wrote down the vital events with, I suppose, their slightly arthritic hands gripping goose-feather pens. A page from the early part of the chronicle reads:

> *Sixty winters ere that Christ was born, Caius Julius, emperor of the Romans, with eighty ships sought Britain. There he was first beaten in a dreadful fight, and lost a great part of his army.*

The chronicle goes on to describe Julius Caesar moving south to Gaul, where he gathered six hundred ships and returned to Britain, only to be defeated again. This account gives us a feeling that Julius Caesar's famous 'I came, I saw, I conquered' is a mere bluff. A shambolic invasion without much gain.

Then I read more of what the pompous Roman did in this part of the world. In the same entry, it says Caesar finally gained some land '*after much fighting*'. I like the economical use of the seemingly plain language. One can still sense the irony and even the cynicism of certain English monks. The mention of the River Thames strikes me as at once distant and familiar: '*Then took the Welsh sharp piles, and drove them with great clubs into the water, at a certain ford of the river called Thames.*' I wonder in which county or village the monk lived when he was writing this line? Did he have any notion about the River Thames, its colour and its estuary flows? Or was it as unfamiliar to him as a river called Seine or Rhine?

And of course, the Thames was there before the Romans and its waters had been flowing before anyone came onto the scene of history, long before it was named Tamesas, or Tamesis. Still, I am hopelessly caught in a human-centred narrative. I think of my reading experiences in Chinese books, and how frequently the Great Wall of China was mentioned. I used to think that in our recent history, the Industrial Revolution was the most significant event, as it forever altered our way of living. But perhaps my mind was simply unable to go back further. Anything further than that, and history feels like fable or myth. Whereas something like the Industrial Revolution is real and tangible. Traces of that particular history are still visible to us, and we can feel its continued presence in our living experiences. That history is not remote at all. Living in a rusty part of England, I can easily touch the scruffy surfaces of objects from two hundred or three hundred years ago. The iron railings right beside me as I walk along the old Hastings Pier; the metal staircase leading up to Hastings Castle; the rusty construction of an amusement park in front of the White Rock Hotel – all that feels concrete and corporeal.

But let me pull back my thoughts and return to the chronicle. Those stoic medieval monks described the cowardly Romans in effective wording: '*they would not go over the ford*'. What a laconic description. I also find it amusing. Despite the Romans' ambition, how timid and clueless those foreigners were in a land of stinging nettles and rains! They missed too much of their wine and figs and melons and olives and sunny afternoons! If the chroniclers had known what a Mediterranean life was like for the Romans, they might have written this entry differently.

Builder Andy

All is quiet. Even the tide below my windows seems motionless. I wait. Last week when the builder Andy came to the flat, he promised he would return this morning by nine o'clock. When I offered him a tea with milk and sugar, he stirred the tea bag with a spoon and remarked with gratitude: 'This is a real cup of tea.' He stressed the word 'real'. Yes, it was a real mug of English tea: full milk not skimmed, two sugars not one, a proper big mug with the face of the current English queen. (The mug was from a charity shop, it cost five pence.) 'I'm quite busy these next few months – all the Polish have left. But I'll see what I can do.' I nodded understandingly. I watched him drink the tea, both of us suddenly wordless. I wished the tea was not so hot, so that he could finish it sooner. A real cup of tea. He measured my windows and announced he would come with tools and materials next time. He was precise, and concise. I had total trust in his words. He told me the estimated cost for replacing the windows. The price seemed reasonable.

Today he doesn't show up.

I decide to wait a bit longer. Maybe a two-hour delay is normal for a busy builder from Essex or Sussex. He might be very popular. I met Andy in a paint shop two weeks ago. I was there to look for painting materials for my walls: brushes, rollers, trays, sandpaper and an extension pole. I mistook Andy for the salesperson as he looked totally at home in the place. 'No, I am not the shopkeeper, but I would say you really don't want to get this type of brush.' He recommended a different brush. I immediately took his advice. Then I asked him about different types of paint, though I was determined to choose my preferred colour. He bought two rollers. We both paid and left. It was pouring outside and we stood by the door, waiting. I asked him if he would by any chance have time to replace the windows in my flat. I realised my question must seem odd. I explained to him that my flat was too dreary and needed simple improvement. Surprisingly, he said yes. I was thrilled. Are builders along the English coast always so spontaneous and friendly? I didn't dare ask roughly how much it might cost. He would give me a quote once he had seen my place. To thank him, I bought him a cup of automatic machine coffee, which was right outside the paint shop. It was drizzling. He left his card and waved in a jolly way. Off he drove in his white van. I studied his card as the rain slowly receded. I decided to call him right away.

Now I trace all these details of meeting Andy, as if he is the most important person in Hastings for me. It's sort of true, he is very important, especially when so many foreign workers have left Britain and I know no other builder who can repair my flat.

The Waves

Today is the white pale blue after last night's mild storm. I stare into the water. When I look at the ceaseless waves, I think of King Cnut.

King Cnut reigned nineteen years before Harold became king. He bore a fine title – King of England, Denmark and Norway. That's a hell of a claim, as grand as a Roman emperor. The most humorous story about this northern king concerns the waves and the tides. It is said that when King Cnut was at the height of his power, he ordered his chair to be placed on the beach. Then he said to the rising tide, something like the following: 'I sit here on my land, this land is mine. You are therefore subject to me. Do not rise against me. I command you, therefore, you impish waves, do not rise on to my land, nor to presume to wet my fine clothing, even less the delicate and shapely limbs of your master.' But still the sea came up, and drenched the king's feet, and his fine robe. Leaving his chair, and retreating from the water, the king cried out: 'Send word to all that the power of kings is vain. There is no king deserving of the name except for Him, by whose will heaven, earth and the sea obey eternal laws.'

I have always liked this rather childlike fable. Is it possible that the rising tides wetting King Cnut's feet produced a sudden illumination? Might a seemingly simple fact have made him wiser? Like Buddha discovering the truth of life under the Bodhi tree, or Newton seeing an apple falling to the ground.

If you stare at the waves long enough, the voices in your head either disappear or become madder and madder. Or at least the voices in my head. I keep Virginia Woolf's *The Waves* by my bedside. Occasionally, I read a few lines before I go to sleep. But the voices in her book won't stop. The voices in her book are constant streams of madness. I am not sure if they grow madder as the book progresses. I feel each voice is equally mad, and consistent. But all this madness can be summed up in one line. It is somewhere in the middle of the novel. It is roughly: 'The authentics exist most completely in solitude.'

Virginia Woolf was an authentic who was able to express herself only in solitude. As do all her maddening voices and characters. I wonder if her characters would think and speak differently if they lived by this part of the Channel in current times. The times and the place are so much more cosmopolitan and open than in Woolf's war years. But at the same time, for a woman writer or an immigrant artist, little has changed. With financial pressures and family duties weighing upon me, not a day passes when I feel easy-going or complacent about the solitude I have managed to find. Solitude is something very special. It is a fragile state of being. It is almost antisocial, requiring a constant and reflexive rejection of what passes for 'life' – that unceasing entanglement with people, domesticity and institutional roles. To be solitary means to be self-sufficient enough to live outside of that world. And as a writer, I feel that I am constantly trying to create this solitude while at the same time coping with its downsides. I am not so different from the eternal waves on the sea, ceaselessly moving and troubled, like Woolf's mad and maddening voices.

Fifty-Three Winters

Reading the *Anglo-Saxon Chronicle* is a curious experience. I like the style of 'this year someone did that and this year someone else did that'. Neither scholarly nor contrived. It's the best bedtime reading material. It creates coherent dream sequences after I fall asleep. The dreams are full of narratives. One such dream occurred in my bed in Hastings. A nameless king is slain by his brother's wife who, although in a sexual relationship with the king, wants her husband to succeed to the throne so that her son can become ruler of the country in time. At one point I realised that I was that power-hungry woman. I am not sure if my character spoke in the Anglo-Saxon language or in Chinese. I would never find out.

But the *Anglo-Saxon Chronicle* is not quite a narrative, nor is the prose designed to be beautiful. Whatever beauty we find in the prose is the accidental effect of age, or history. Its voices resemble those of journalists at the front, reporting on the progress of a war and its casualties, no time to mess about. Still, I find it incredible to read a paragraph like this in the chronicle:

> A.D. 560. *This year Ceawlin undertook the government of the West-Saxons; and Ella, on the death of Ida, that of the Northumbrians; each of whom reigned thirty winters. Ella was the son of Iff, Iff of Usfrey, Usfrey of Wilgis, Wilgis of Westerfalcon, Westerfalcon of Seafowl, Seafowl of Sebbald, Sebbald of Sigeat, Sigeat of*

Swaddy, Swaddy of Seagirt, Seagar of Waddy, Waddy of Woden, Woden of Frithowulf.

Such a rapid pace, such a busy listing! Yet what comes from the writing hand of these few monks is History, even if it can only be challenged by sceptical minds.

Names and places, such as 'West-Saxons' are still relevant to current England. For some reason, I am fascinated by such names: Essex, Sussex, Middlesex, Wessex (no longer a shire). The sounds are very exotic to Chinese ears. Once I visited a town in Suffolk called Saxmundham, and I could not get over its ancient name. Saxmundham means Saxon-world-village. Very grand indeed, even though the town was very small. I wandered its plain streets, trying to discover an ancient relic that might capture my attention. Eventually, after hours of wandering, I was so weary I entered the large Tesco to replenish my energy.

An enormous amount of information is contained in those lines filled with names and places. But I am not that bothered by 'Ella was the son of Iff, Iff of Usfrey, Usfrey of Wilgis, Wilgis of Westerfalcon, Westerfalcon of Seafowl, Seafowl of Sebbald, Sebbald of Sigeat . . .' A certain monk from a certain monastery might have consumed quite a quantity of cider or ale when he wrote this. Or he might have been in a huge hurry to get the year's record done, since he was still at AD 560, and his goal for the day was to get to at least AD 620. The day was short and the monastery was cold. He just had to move through time and space without any sentimental attachment to deep truth or knowledge.

In the same entry, the text continues:

This year Ethelbert came to the kingdom of the Cantuarians, and held it fifty-three winters. In his days the holy Pope Gregory sent us baptism. That was in the two and thirtieth year of his reign. And Columba, the mass-priest, came to the Picts, and converted them to the belief of Christ . . . There he was abbot two and thirty winters; and there he died, when he was seventy-seven years old.

I am more interested in expressions such as 'thirty winters', 'fifty-three winters' and 'seventy-seven years' than in those innumerable names. It feels melancholic, even mournful to record the passage of time by counting winters. I remind myself that Britain is a northern country with long winters. Counting them is something significant, and perhaps it effectively conveys the feeling of endless cold nights. Men and women only age if they have endured enough winters. Like the Chinese counting the full moons, the Saxons count the winters to measure living time.

Spring

Saxons / Tang

The trees are still leafless, though their green buds are trying to open in the cold. Only the blackberry and gooseberry bushes send out their thorny shoots on the roadsides. April is definitely the cruellest month in Britain. T. S. Eliot nailed it after living in England for several years as an American. Perhaps a foreigner knows more about his adopted land than the locals, because a foreigner feels more acutely the particularities of a new environment. I have never adapted to English weather, at least not so far. As the gloomy days of March passed in snowflakes and frost, I imagined the weather would improve soon, that I would be able to survive in my cold Hastings flat. But April has arrived, and it is even colder. In the flat I wear a padded coat and wool trousers and woolly slippers. I read the *Anglo-Saxon Chronicle* to pass the time. I hope to understand the year 1066, and the events around that period, which, I am told, shaped England to this day. I don't think many of the locals care much about the remote past of Hastings and the surrounding areas. But I cannot be so complacent. I don't like to think of myself as a selfish and indifferent immigrant, even though I can be selfish and indifferent in many other ways. It's simply that I wouldn't feel good about owning a home in a foreign town without understanding its past, even though that past is so distant it may as well be a myth, a hyperbolic narrative belonging only in some expensive production from Netflix.

So I turn my attention to that period. In China, if we want to mention a high cultural point of history, we say, 'It's like the Tang Dynasty.' Mostly, this would be said with a sigh by old people: 'It will never be as good as in the days of Tang, when the country was wealthy and people were content . . .' Tang culture was more than a thousand years ago, and it ended around AD 900, before the Battle of Hastings. A god in the heavens would get a good picture of that time by looking to the east and then looking to the west. He would see that during the landscape-painting and flower-worshipping Tang period, the old Saxons were still the dominant power in England, though England was not yet a concept. Vikings and Normans were not yet in charge. I wonder if the locals said the same thing after the Norman Conquest. 'It is not as good as in old Saxon days,' they might have said bitterly, thinking of their family, slaughtered by the Normans. 'The old kingdom of Wessex has gone.' Perhaps the Anglo-Saxons sighed sorrowfully, just like old Chinese people.

But even during those good old days, killing was everywhere and every day. Violence was the reality of life. I, too, come from a history of violence, probably an even more extreme one. In the eighth century, the An Lushan Rebellion killed 36 million people in China, one-fifth of the world population at the time. Killing occurred by hand in ancient times, slaughtering one by one – it takes a huge amount of energy and effort. To slaughter one million would be an immense task, let alone 36 million.

I open a page in the *Anglo-Saxon Chronicle*, around the same period as the Tang Dynasty in China:

> A.D. 780. *This year a battle was fought between the Old-Saxons and the Franks; and the high-sheriffs of Northumbria committed to the flames . . .*
>
> A.D. 784. *This year Cyneard slew King Cynewulf, and was slain himself, and eighty-four men with him. Then Bertric undertook the government of the West-Saxons, and reigned sixteen years. His body is deposited at Wareham . . .*

*A.D. 789. This year Elwald, king of the Northumbrians, was
slain by Siga . . .*

*A.D. 792. This year Offa, King of Mercia, commanded that
King Ethelbert should be beheaded; and Osred, who had been
king of the Northumbrians, returning home after his exile, was
apprehended and slain . . .*

The relentlessly violent, almost apocalyptic nature of the period
dominates many parts of the chronicle. It is such a contrast to our
life now, at least for people living in peacetime. The more one reads
about history, the more one questions the nature of peace. A great
danger seems to lurk behind times of peace, as though the great fire
can be ignited from a tiny local eruption in the middle of night.

The entry right after AD 792 in the chronicle records other
forms of violence:

*A.D. 793. This year came dreadful fore-warnings over the land of
the Northumbrians, terrifying the people most woefully: these
were immense sheets of light rushing through the air, and whirl-
winds, and fiery dragons flying across the firmament. These
tremendous tokens were soon followed by a great famine.*

What are these 'immense sheets of light rushing through the air'?
And what are the 'fiery dragons flying across the firmament'? Natural
phenomena, in the eyes of medieval people? They must have believed
that creatures like 'fiery dragons' truly existed. Given that paganism
was still around in post-Roman Britain, what did they think of God's
relation to a fiery dragon? Or indeed, God's relation to any mon-
strous creatures? Was God manifested as a fiery dragon? In China, a
dragon is the highest-ranking creature in the animal-sign hierarchy.
In imperial China, no one except for the emperor could use the
dragon symbol or image. The emperor alone was permitted to have
the dragon on his house, clothing and personal items. I wonder when
people stopped believing in such a creature, even if tribal peoples

somewhere continue to believe in dragons or sea monsters. I notice that most Chinese dragons are wingless, while the Western ones have wings.

Once again, the chronicle documents the savagery of the Vikings, '*the harrowing inroads of heathen men made lamentable havoc in the church of God in Holy-island, by rapine and slaughter*'. Holy Island is Lindisfarne in Scotland, a place I need to visit one day. But the concept of 'heathen men' is difficult for Chinese people to grasp since Chinese societies have never been as religiously controlled as European ones, nor has any church in China dominated state power the way it has in the West. In that sense, the idea of heathen men, pagans, Christians or non-Christians has no significance for a non-religious Chinese person. But I must not look for excuses. I am living in the West and speaking one of their tongues. I must commit myself to learning all the differences as though I am in a re-education camp, even if this re-education camp enrols people voluntarily and without a room of concrete walls. Either you are in the society or you are out. You have no choice if you are an immigrant and particularly if you are a non-white non-European.

In a historical narrative such as the chronicle, I find myself unable to separate metaphors from facts, myths from reality. I understand only the phrase 'rapine and slaughter', a straightforward description of violence. Almost reflexively, I picture Putin's armies beginning a new military operation by bombing Western Europe, no food in the supermarket, no children in schools, nobody in the streets of Germany or France or Britain. People are either hiding or dead, and there are only soldiers and tanks, smoke and ruins.

Normans

For the English, on one side of the Channel, the Normans were the enemy. But the Duke of Normandy was a family member of the English king. Cousins. Brothers. Feuds and enmities. Always the same. Europe is a closely knit family. Wasn't the last tsar of Russia the brother of the last kaiser of Germany as well as the cousin of King George of England? Always the same. Power remains within the family, even though everyone tries to get rid of the ones stepping on their toes. Still, here we are talking about a thousand years ago. Mad Europe, raging wars and the awful tribalism which humans are so good at engaging in.

The Normans were from Normandy and beyond. A thousand years ago, globalism did not exist. If there was anything structuring society, it was tribalism. 'Who are the Normans?' I imagine a student asking her teacher in class. 'The Normans,' the teacher answers, 'are also called Norsemen or Northmen. They are a loose collection of northern Germanic groups.'

When we think of Vikings, the cliché from the movies comes to mind: a violent sea people, sailing forth in interesting-looking boats to plunder food and goods from agricultural lands far from their home. Yet everyone seems to be linked to Vikings. William the Conqueror was a descendant of Rollo, the Viking who founded Normandy. On the other side of the English Channel, Harold Godwinson's mother Gytha was Danish, part of the family of King

Cnut, the ruler of the North Sea Empire. I have a sense that much literature has been written about the Vikings, all charged with pride and myth, but not so much about the Normans. My understanding is that we are fascinated with the more violent group who managed to conquer the less violent group.

Anglo-Normans. That's a good word, a useful word. It suggests the composite nature of one of the populations around this part of the coast in olden times. Of course, I never hear anyone use it now, in our day-to-day life. Our DNA has demonstrated all possible inceptions for our people. We can have one and many origins at the same time. Even for a villager like me, born in a totally enclosed Chinese peasant place, I, too, am a mix of bloods and genes. I am of mixed race. My father's family was Hakka Hui, of Muslim origin, and my mother's family was Han Chinese. I am a daughter of the Confucian tradition with a Communist upbringing. I speak Hakka and Mandarin, as well as European languages. I share many things with everyone in this world. But apparently, we humans also share 60 per cent of our DNA with a banana. How arbitrary is that? Half of our genes have counterparts in bananas! We are just a bunch of very complicated and violent bananas. Neither Vikings nor Anglo-Normans can escape their relation to bananas, even if the Vikings probably never tasted or saw a banana in their time.

Baby Goose Drops

In Hastings I wake up early. There are no curtains in this flat, and dawn light from above the sea illuminates the room as early as the sun rises. Still, I prefer not to have curtains. The simpler the flat is, the better. This is some kind of odd decision I have made for this place. There is no television, internet or washing machine either. I bought a small fridge, but it remains unplugged. In fact, its electric cord is still wrapped up. Hopefully it will never need to be unwrapped. Minimal. No cost of any energy, apart from my own. I prefer that. Not quite a stone age, but a stone-age life in the twenty-first century.

This weekend I have my child Moon and her father Steve with me. Steve likes to be by the sea as well as swimming in it, whether it's a cold northern sea or a warm one. Moon is not sure about the cold English sea yet. She is a nine-year-old and does not like to get wet from the icy water. This morning, all of us get up around seven. We gather in the same room by the window, looking out at the sea bathed in the morning light. Just staring, doing nothing. Sunlight is coming in, with its silent cosmic vibration. Each minute is brighter, and stronger. Clouds are slowly moving away, leaving the sky in vast blue. We can see the tide receding, or is it actually coming in? I am confused. Technically it is low tide, according to the local paper, the *Hastings Daily*. We notice two lines of geese in a V-shaped formation, flying towards the south. Perhaps they are migrating? Their symmetric shape is so perfect and elegant, as though they have rehearsed this a hundred times for a movie scene. The ones heading in the front seem to be bigger birds, and they fly higher. The ones on the end of the line look smaller, flying low, just above the water. The group passes in front of us, flapping; quickly they disappear in the corner of our window view. But in no time, another V-shaped group appears. They also fly from north to south, all flapping their wings, all synchronised, all balanced in perfect unison. It is beautiful to watch, and mysterious to understand. How do they perform so well in a team? Do they all know where they are heading to? Do they improvise sometimes on their path? Say, a leading goose decides to descend, coming down and taking a break, do the rest then follow? Or what if the leading bird takes a U-turn, for some reason – will the rest continue along the old route or follow the U-turn?

'They are flapping differently: this one is doing up and down, that one is doing down and up! They are not doing the same thing, Dad,' Moon observes.

I get up and go to the kitchen for more coffee. Steve is taking the job of answering questions:

'That's right. Whenever a bird flies directly behind another, it will reverse the flapping pattern. So that it can counter the down-wash force to lift itself upwards.'

'Really? That's so clever . . .' The child is in awe.

I come back with two coffees, and join them again for the collective staring. Suddenly Moon cries out:

'Look, Daddy! The little one is behind! The last one is falling far behind . . . it is going to drop!!!'

We all look up. Yes, it's true, the very last goose has just created a big gap from the V-shaped flight. It is flapping its wings in a nervous way, and it is sinking down towards the water surface. While the rest of the team just fly forward, not noticing anything wrong. They are moving further and further away. It is a cruel thing to watch, for a nine-year-old.

'The little baby bird is going to die! No . . . he is being left alone!'

Bursting into tears, Moon puts her palms over her eyes. Steve and I watch the little bird dropping straight down towards the wavy sea. We put our hands on Moon's shoulder, we do not want her to see this. 'Is the little goose flying again? Is he following?' Moon asks through her firmly closed palms. As I look again at the drowning bird, all I can see now are the churning waves. The V-shaped team has moved towards a new horizon where my eyes cannot follow.

'Yes, the little bird has managed to catch up again,' I say. 'Yes, it is flying together with the big ones. Now they have gone. All gone now.'

Moon stops crying, moving her palms away from her eyes. She stares at the sea, searching for the goose. But there are only waves. Only the blue sky. Everything is illuminated. All is peaceful.

When a beam of sunlight moves in between the window frames, I notice the child's tears are wet on her face.

Land of Hope and Kippers

Everyone loathes Boris Johnson, the current prime minister, and wants him to resign. This seems to be a fact even within the Conservative Party. I wonder when he will stand down. Perhaps very soon? But how soon? I don't understand how British politics works. Sometimes, it seems, a prime minister stays in their position forever despite the fact everyone is appalled by their behaviour, others leave in the middle of their time in office just because of some private matter being exposed by the media. All this feels arbitrary and unstable for a foreigner like me. But maybe that is how democracy works? A memorable moment for me about Boris Johnson was a piece of news last year, which was broadcast as Breaking News one morning, when I was still looking for a place to live by the English Channel. The news said: *US lift ban on British lambs, says Boris Johnson.*

At first, I thought, why is this considered breaking news? Was selling lambs especially significant? Why was there a ban from the all-powerful USA in the first place? I still remember reading about mad cow disease in the UK in the 1990s, and British sheep have been linked to scrapie, a neurodegenerative disease from long ago. But I was not aware that their export had been banned ever since. I listened to more news, and learned that the prime minister just went to the US and made a trade deal with President Biden. Now British farmers could export meat to the US for 'the first time in decades'. So, it is a big deal then.

This made me think of the British national fish – smoked kippers. But my image of the fish is tightly wrapped in a plastic bag. In a post-Brexit speech broadcast on BBC Television a few years ago, Johnson raised a smoked kipper proudly onstage while making his speech. According to him, kippers are one of our national treasures and have everlasting trade value. The way he raised the fish in its plastic bag with such force was beyond comic. It was heroic in a tragic way. It is not an appropriate comparison, but the scene reminded me of Martin Luther King raising his arm in front of a crowd and stating: 'I have a dream.'

In Johnson's case, 'I have a fish.' And he will swim, back and forth, in the sea of politics. Could any woman politician have done that? I mean, tell lie after lie? No. That requires male privilege and entitlement. Margaret Thatcher stated: 'There is no such thing as society,' and 'There is no alternative.' When she spoke, people were convinced that she was committed to what she was saying, and that was important to people. Her appeal was forthright truthfulness, even if a harsh 'truth'. But Johnson was clearly not committed to his words. His words were delivered with a smirk on his face. That did not matter for his appeal; in fact it was part of it. The alpha male at the top of the social pile can smirk, and that reassures those lower down that all must be well. I cannot imagine Alfred the Great delivered his speech in that way.

Burning Wild Fens

I have always believed myself to be an unsophisticated person in relation to Western cultures, with their ancient histories. Firstly, this was due to my limited Chinese Communist education when I lived in my province. Secondly, being a foreigner and an Asian makes my understanding of Europe, especially Anglo-Saxon history, difficult. To my Chinese mind, the word Anglo-Saxon meant 'medieval', and it effectively reduced Western civilisation into a dim picture of bearded churchmen dressed in robes, reading or writing next to a feebly burning candle. After I came to Britain, I discovered the existence of those large historical records, such as the *Anglo-Saxon Chronicle* and the Domesday Book, and the immediate association for me was the Chinese equivalent, the book of *Shiji*. *Shiji*, translated as *Records of the Grand Historian*, was written by Sima Qian two thousand years ago. It records similar events to those in the *Anglo-Saxon Chronicle* in ancient China. Another book, *Erya*, was composed around 3 BC, and is the first Chinese dictionary as well as an encyclopedia. *Erya* has been translated as *The Literary Expositor*, or *The Semantic Approximator*, according to different sinologists. Both *Shiji* and *Erya* are impossible for modern Chinese people to read or understand because they are written in ancient Chinese script. All the same, they are mysterious and attractive to me. It is as though those ancient records hold the truth of our past, the essence of our identity without having been altered by censorship or manipulated by the ruling powers. This is naive thinking, I know, but for someone like me, growing up under the heavy censorship of the Communist regime, I cannot help but have more faith in the ancient records than the modern ones. Perhaps that is why in a second-hand bookshop in St Leonards I opened a random page of the chronicle and was struck by what I read of how the Vikings raided England:

> For three months they plundered and burned, and then proceeded further into the wild fens. And they burned Thetford and Cambridge and then went southward to the Thames and those who were mounted rode towards the ships and then turned westward toward to Oxfordshire and thence to Buckinghamshire and so along the Ouse until they came to Bedford and so forth to Temsford and burned everything where they went. Then they went to their ships with their plunder.

The text, with its straightforward tone, was somehow mesmerising to me. I didn't even realise it was a modern translation of the ancient version. But I was a beginner of this culture, and I was on a quest to know more about the Anglo-Saxons beyond the current United Kingdom. I decided to buy the copy. I looked at the price. A faint pencil mark scribbled on the second page: £2.50. That was what history was worth. How generous, and underwhelming at the same time.

As I walked home with the book under my arm, I could not help but think of the 'burning wild fens'. Fens – an unfamiliar word for me, not ferns. I checked its origin. It is Germanic, related to Dutch *veen* and German *Fenn*. I read those mysterious lines again: '*For three months they plundered and burned, and then proceeded further into the wild fens. And they burned Thetford and Cambridge and then went southward to the Thames . . .*' A series of powerful images were forming in my head as I walked past the grey shore.

Burning wild fens. I could not get these words out of my head.

Incredible. But in my experience Britain is always inked with deep green and splashed with rains, burning the land would be difficult. And it was probably even wetter and colder a thousand years ago when Vikings raided the isles. In the wetland of Britain, wild *ferns*, not *fens*, would grow lushly everywhere. So strong were their stems, they must have been hard to get rid of, even if the Vikings were endlessly burning the land. Wheat fields and orchards might not have survived after months plundering. Or, perhaps, one summer afternoon a thousand years ago, the sky was blue and the sun hot. Ferns, nettles, barley, corn, wheat, beets, potatoes, fruit trees on English hills might be set alight like being caught in a desert fire. They could burn from the Kent coast to Norfolk, or from Blackpool to Yorkshire. All of them were being torched by the brutes.

But one thousand years have passed now, most of those brutes have become very civilised. They have become tree lovers and land conservationists. It is only a matter of time, though a matter of a long, long time.

Veni, Vidi, Vici

Perhaps the most concise and powerful war slogan in human history is from Julius Caesar: Veni, vidi, vici. It's even good in English: I came, I saw, I conquered. This phrase – I came, I saw, I conquered – is also what the Normans did when they came down to Britain. The phrase sums up the prose style of the *Anglo-Saxon Chronicle* too. The clerks did not use the first-person point of view, but the matter-of-fact and non-sentimental tone is nearly the same.

A similar phrase could have described my way of coming to England from China: I came, I saw, I wrote.

This seems to sum up my life in the West. Rarely is there a week or even a day where I fail to write down what I see in my daily life. Perhaps in some way I have tried to conquer, to win a world that will allow me to do things that I always wanted to, or live in the best way I can. But conquering is a short-lived act, and it can never hope to endure in any future. We have to continually conquer because circumstances change, and time moves forward. All is in flux. One can never remain in a static 'conquered' world. Even Julius Caesar was assassinated, in a most brutal way, by his own men.

But perhaps I should describe my existence in the West more precisely. I should perhaps change the phrase to: I came, I saw, I wandered.

Yes, apart from writing, all I have done is wander. Wandering around all the time even after my own child was born. Wandering every day in all seasons. This morning, I wandered for a long time. Starting from the pier, I took a long walk towards the White Rock Theatre, turning upwards to the hills and passing the swimming pool and the fields. I walked up to the west, passing St Leonards Garden. I noticed hyacinth blooming, its strong odour filling the air, and daffodils that were mostly dead. I walked up the Maze Hill towards Crowhurst Road, past rows of brick houses with their small front gardens, and oak and ash trees. I met hardly anyone on that road. Then I found myself on Church Wood looking down at the sea and the town. The view up there never disappoints me. From high above, even a sad and shabby town looks pretty and poetic. By the time I got to Ingleside I felt my knees were hurting. I turned back, descending the zigzag hilly streets and returning home. I must sit down to write, I told myself. I am here in Hastings to write, otherwise I would have to return to London, taking care of my child and my partner, surrendering to the domestic.

To be able to wander around freely is a luxury. To be able to write without domestic duties is even more of a luxury. Perhaps a man doesn't feel these things are precious, at least not as acutely as I do. I still remember the first three years after my child was born. I was unable to sleep more than three or four hours a night. During those years I was unable to think, never mind write. I also felt totally isolated from my social life, which seemed to have vanished instantly. Several years have passed, and I am recovering from that state of being. But now I feel an urgency to recapture the years I lost. To do so, I have to sometimes live alone, without my child or my partner, and this aloneness is something I have to protect and pursue, even if at the same time I suffer the disapproving gaze of other mothers.

Rating Certificate

Every evening, the wind from the north sends a persistent signal. The seafront buildings are under constant assault from the fast-moving atmosphere. The windows in my flat are clattering. Draught travels through the space from one end to the other. Every wall is icy. Every crack on the window frames invites more cold. The worst is the soggy bathroom, so small there is no room to install a radiator. I read the energy rating of the flat before purchasing it. But it was still abstract for me then, even though the rating certificate was frank about its appalling insulation. Well, one would presume that an energy performance certificate implies that the flat is qualified for standard living, and therefore it is legal to sell. But obviously this is not the case. Now I find this certificate in one of the drawers. I pin it on the kitchen wall so I can read it properly:

Rating explained:

Each feature is assessed as one of the following:

1. Very good (most efficient)
2. Good
3. Average
4. Poor
5. Very poor (least efficient)

The page comes with three columns:

Feature	Description	Ratings
Wall timber frame	As built, no insulation (assumed)	Very poor
Roof pitched	No insulation (assumed)	Very poor
Window	Partial double glazing	Poor
Main heating	Electric storage heaters	Average
Main heating control	Manual	Average to poor
Hot water	Electric immersion	Average

I study the word: *assumed*. Is that even an official word they use for an energy certificate? I imagine the man who assessed this place with whatever tools he had (indeed, a pair of naked eyes) 'assumed' the ratings about the roof and wall timber. One could assume anything without the trouble of going up on the roof or examining the inner wall structure. One could even assume this house was built partially with marble or anything a construction team would have used. I *assume* the building had its glorious days, and now each item on the energy performance is poor, or very poor. To be average is an achievement. To be good is unbelievable.

I also become aware of a more serious matter. A fire assessment risk. I am on the top floor of a very old building. The only escape route during a fire for me is via the communal interior staircase.

Unless I plunge myself onto the pavement next to the sea from my fourth-floor window. I read the fire hazard notice too:

> *In the event of fire, all flats except for the basement and top floors:*
>
> *You should ensure that a lobbied approach is provided to all entrances, which shall be so configured that any risk in the flat shall be separated from the protected escape route by means of two 30mm fire resisting doors.*

I am not sure what 'a lobbied approach' consists of, since there is no lobby in the building. There is only a single entrance leading to the upstairs flats. All communal spaces are being used. Even the cupboard on the landing with the gas meters is cramped with cleaning stuff.

This much is clear: I live in a cheap loft construction without a proper fire door or safe exit. To make the situation worse, I am right above the shop with hot ovens that cook pizza all day long. The people who work in the takeaway do long hours. They could doze off during a shift and let a fire envelop the building.

The Strait of Dover

The Strait of Dover, especially at the Channel's eastern end, is the narrowest point between Britain and France. In French, this part is called Pas de Calais. Because it is narrow, it has gathered more sediment on the seabed than other parts of the Channel. The water is relatively shallow, the average depth around 120 metres, whereas the rest of the Channel reaches 170 metres.

But still, this is the North Sea coast, part of the Atlantic. Everywhere along this coastline shares a similarly harsh seascape: rugged and eroded land, salt marsh and low-lying vegetation. Standing at the top of any hill in Hastings or Bexhill or Brighton, you can feel that harshness, even on a mild sunny day. I recently read a report published by some geologists that said the seascape in this part of the world is recognisably similar to the seascape from a thousand years ago. That's remarkable. I can almost picture the vivid seascape during the Battle of Hastings by looking at the current one.

High wind since yesterday. The wind is not directly from the Channel. It comes from the north and turns anticlockwise until the water is churned up like an enormous pregnant oyster. One of the local papers, the *Hastings Independent*, reports that there were migrant boats yesterday carrying 1,500 refugees trying to cross the Channel. Did they arrive at Dover? The news doesn't say. What it does say clearly is that the Border Police were authorised to turn the boat back to the French side. So, does it mean 1,500 people have been turned back into the Channel? Or is that confidential information, which won't be revealed to the public? I have learned that once migrants land on English soil (after being received by the Border Police) they can claim asylum status in the UK. So the government clearly wants to turn the boat back to French waters.

But everyone in Britain knows there has been a shortage of migrant workers in the country. There are not enough truck drivers, not enough fruit pickers, not enough builders, and not enough nurses and doctors. The government prefers that its citizens don't have fresh vegetables and fruit, or a choice of European products in their shops.

I listen to more news on the radio. There is a dispute about the behaviour of the British Border Police. When they turn back the migrant boats towards French water, they need the consent of the French to do so. Apparently the French have already refused this plan and are simply not engaging with them. So, everyone wonders, what will happen with the boat and the refugees? How long can a boat remain in international waters? Until everyone is drowned? And only at the drowning point will there be an official 'rescue' by police on one side or the other? According to the *Daily Mail*, Britain has already paid nearly half a billion pounds to France in the preceding decade to help tackle migration. And the government will be paying another half-billion to France in the subsequent years building detention centres on the Continent. As an exercise of thought I imagine this 'half-billion' being used on rescuing drowning refugees every year, and on helping migrants to become part of communities by the Channel. Perhaps we would gain a much better economic outcome doing this than sending money abroad to stop the boats coming in the first place. Perhaps next time I need a plumber or a builder, there would be one available who could come and help quickly.

I think of 'Dover Beach' by Matthew Arnold. The final lines sum up my feeling about the immigrants on the boats during the night, before they become the morning news on the radio and in the paper:

> *And we are here as on a darkling plain*
> *Swept with confused alarms of struggle and flight,*
> *Where ignorant armies clash by night.*

The beach is one of the first battlegrounds. In my Chinese village Shitang by the Taiwan Strait, mainlanders would leave secretly on their boat at night in order to get to Taiwan, a supposed free land on the other side of the water, only to be shot at by soldiers when they reached the international waters. As a child I heard of so many villagers being shot right on their boats. But some succeeded. The beaches of Shitang were also a place of mourning for our village widows. Those wives never saw but always watched for their husbands returning – some died from the storms, some from reasons never known. I know my childhood beaches. And I know my childhood sea.

Yet as I walk on these shingle stones, I see nothing, hear nothing. Only the wind, the waves, the unbearable forgetfulness of history.

Haestingas

The word *Haestingas* sounds how a French speaker might pronounce the English word *Hastings*, stressing the ending – *ings*. But it is a Germanic word. Haestingas was the name of a tribe that lived in south-east England from the fourth or fifth century. Of course, at that time, the concept of 'England' didn't exist yet. But the Haestingas inhabited an area of land that spanned the east of Sussex to the west part of Kent.

I first come across the word during a visit to the Hastings Museum. My child and her father are staying for the weekend and we head to the museum because of an animal origami workshop, which Moon is interested in.

The museum is a century-old red-brick building in the hilly part of the town. The collection of local treasures is carefully curated. There is even a dinosaur gallery! It's more like a cabinet of curiosities than a museum. The ground floor exhibits the artefacts of local history with a grand title: *History of Hastings: from the Stone Age to Modern Days*. This is about a history before Anglo-Saxon culture became entrenched. It's at this moment I learn where the name 'Hastings' comes from.

The Haestingas were an early Saxon people originally from the Baltic Sea area. The records trace them to the third century or even before. Eventually they were assimilated into the Kingdom of Wessex, in the ninth century. So the Haestingas were some kind of 'original' English people if you like, or one of the 'original' Anglo-Saxon tribes. But 'original' is not the right word here. There were people living on the land before the Haestingas, before the Vikings, before the Romans, before the Celts. We can reach back to our cousins the Neanderthals if we have to.

I picture the old Haestingas dressed in coats made of fern and bark, and they would dance in the forest during the summer in the way the ancient farmers would dance in old England, and sing songs about animals and their pagan gods. They would have never imagined that the modern Haestingas would be mainly made up of income-deprived families who could not afford heating bills or basic food, resigned to passing the hours in front of the television on their musty sofas.

By the time Moon finishes crafting five origami animals, Steve and I are still only halfway through the migration history of Haestingas. I have learned that the Haestingas tribe was composed of a mix of people, mainly Ingaevonic (ancient people from north-west Germany) and Aesti (ancient people from what is modern-day Sweden). But I must slow down, I feel as though I have eaten a heavy meal and I cannot digest what's in my stomach. There is so much to take in, even in the history of a small place like this. There is tribe after tribe: Ingaevonic, Aesti, Franks, Jutes, and many more. My head swims with the names. But I am sure of this. All these tribes wanted to do the same thing: to survive. History is about the stomach and how it gets fed, whether by migration or conquest. A full stomach is happiness, as we Chinese say. I am not sure whether the modern Hastingaes live more happily than did the ancient Hastingaes. The modern stomach still groans from the scarcities of our time.

When I think of the part of old England where the Haestingas supposedly lived, I think of a mythical creature, a dragon-like thing, called a wyvern. It often appears in fantasy literature and video games. I must have read about wyvern in some fables after I came to England. A wyvern is a two-legged dragon. It is not fire-breathing like in Chinese legends, rather it has a watery quality. It is like a winged snake, or a flying lizard. That is how I think of the world when old Haestingas tried to survive under attacks from animals and bad weather.

In the evening light, as we walk around the pub-noise-filled streets, our shadows long and lonely under the lamp posts, I think of us three. I realise that we are also a tribe, a little one, 'originally' from somewhere else, some place far away. I am from China, Steve from Australia, but perhaps none of our ancestors are from the land where we were born. And Moon? Where is she from? I look back at the child walking behind us, slowing down as she picks up little stones on the way and plays with a leafless branch she finds somewhere. Perhaps she is from the land of western wyverns and eastern dragons, or from neither of these places. She is from a new world, constructed by elements we sometimes recognise, sometimes not. But still, a relatively new world from ours.

Godwinson

Harold Godwinson, the last Anglo-Saxon king of England, was also a Viking. Or to be more precise, a half Viking. His mother was Danish. Her name was Gytha Thorkelsdóttir. She was linked to the family of the great King Cnut. I wonder whether his mother spoke a version of Danish to him when he was a child, even though child Harold was born in Wessex. What did it mean for a Scandinavian noblewoman to end up in the middle of England, among people who spoke Old English and cooked meals differently? Was wild boar and roasted potatoes their main dish on the dining table? Did the locals prepare fish and bread as the Scandinavians did in the North? And what about the prized jellied eels and smoked kippers in those days? Gytha must have brought plenty of servants with her from Denmark. They might have spoken only Old Norse in the house, since the nobleman Harold Godwin was almost always away. The lords and dukes would have been either hunting or fighting with anyone who threatened their territories. Raids were rampant then, and even a noble family would not be spared. Some of Harold's family went into hiding in Normandy when the Vikings descended upon England.

So what was the 'English' quality, in King Harold's case? Perhaps it has something to do with the land and local armies, and nothing to do with blood. It never really has anything to do with blood. Blood is a false concept. Even the medieval common people knew that. Never mind modern English people, the contemporary population. What on earth were the Brexiteers thinking when they voted for Britain to leave Europe? To gain resources? To gain a sense of lost freedom going back to the era of the Kingdom of Wessex, which had neither freedom nor self-autonomy, but constant wars with invaders and tribal powers? And in any case, 'Anglo-Saxon' is a bastard branding, even if it is honourable all the same. As honourable and arbitrary as any other branding: Mongols, Tatars, Scots, Prussians, Germans, Americans, Chinese. These terms are more political constructs than intrinsically real.

But the birth of the last Anglo-Saxon king in 1022 is not even mentioned in the chronicle. At least I haven't found any reference to it so far. Perhaps the chroniclers simply could not perceive the significance of Harold Godwinson's birth. It was not like the birth of Christ, or the birth of Alfred the Great, who initiated the creation of the *Anglo-Saxon Chronicle* in the ninth century. Those scholars and monks were probably too caught up with the deeds of King Cnut, or the death of some archbishop who they either revered or loathed. To them, the birth of Harold Godwinson was merely a dim moment in a windy, mushroom-growing Saxon forest.

There are only two short entries for the year 1022. Perhaps the churchman who was keeping the record suffered from some lung condition, or terrible malnutrition. As a result, he probably couldn't care less about what happened around the country. Or else during a sleepy evening he was just copying from someone else's record, when a small fire caused by a candle on his desk burned most of the pages, such that he managed to grasp only the remaining half-page and the two events it relates:

A.D. 1022. This year went King Knute out with his ships to the Isle of Wight. And Bishop Ethelnoth went to Rome; where he was received with much honour by Benedict the magnificent pope, who with his own hand placed the pall upon him, and with great pomp consecrated him archbishop, and blessed him, on the nones of October. The archbishop on the self-same day with the same pall performed mass, as the pope directed him, after which he was magnificently entertained by the pope himself; and afterwards with a full blessing proceeded homewards . . .

There is a lot of detail in this entry. Surely any historian or scholar would go crazy for it, with its unusual and emotional descriptive language: magnificent, unjustly, magnificently (for the second time), full, etc. But then I know nothing of abbots or bishops or popes. The equivalents of abbots or bishops or popes in a Chinese Communist Party would be something like: Central Committee, Politburo, the Politburo Standing Committee and the General Secretary of Politburo Committee. Though the Communist Party leaders have no excellent clothing, unlike those abbots and bishops and popes.

I think I understand why some years are so lightly covered by the chroniclers. History is an unbearable burden. An endless repetition of one thing after another. Yet a person's life is short, punctuated by small and big events, before a final illness.

In any case, the published chronicle we have been reading is only a modern translation from Old English. We can hardly trace who translated which version of the original Old English, nor do we even know what was written in the original text. Apparently of the nine manuscripts of the chronicle that survive in whole or in part (mostly now in the British Library and in Oxford), none of them is the original version. So what am I reading, exactly? A heavily manipulated pseudo-history, the fanciful accounts of a bunch of flea-ridden monks in some priory?

Andy Installs Windows

Builder Andy called me yesterday to say the new windows had arrived. Could he bring them and fit them tomorrow? Yes, I said immediately.

The old windows in my flat are in a dreadful state, mouldy and constantly damp because of the rain. The frames rattle noisily every night as I sleep. During the day, too, they shake constantly when the wind is strong. But the damp is the real issue.

'You're not going to get real wooden frames with glass,' Andy informed me when I first asked about the job. 'It's a Brexit supply-chain problem. No truck drivers. We have only plastic windows.'

When I expressed my aesthetic concern about living with plastic windows, he said:

'You won't notice any difference. And aluminium frames, they don't degrade like the wooden ones. They're really solid and can last fifty years or more. With wood you have to replace them every ten years, especially with your building being on the seafront. They get chipped and damaged by storms and rain very easily. They won't last. So what are you after? Long-lasting or short?'

'But are they good for insulation? ' I enquired, without much confidence. 'Are they thick enough?'

'You bet. They're made for insulation. All our windows are double-glazed and come with a maximum thickness of twenty-eight millimetres.'

I did not know much about thickness. If not twenty-eight millimetres, what else? Twenty millimetres? Eighteen millimetres? I needed to study this. But time was short and I also needed to live in a warm flat so I agreed to his proposal. The total cost is £1,900 including labour for replacing all the windows in the three rooms. He does not mention VAT; I presume he will want cash. I decide to prepare cash in any case.

Next morning around nine, after my toast and coffee, I see Andy's white van parking on the pavement below. He disappears from view and the bell rings, while a second man exits the van and opens the back door.

The windows seem to be very heavy. Andy and his man struggle to carry them up. The helper is almost wordless, though when he utters even a monosyllable, he has the same strong accent. He even looks very much like Andy, though at least twenty years younger. Once they get into my flat with all the materials, I serve them two cups of tea. I remember Andy's preference: leaving the tea bag in, full milk, not skimmed, and two spoons of sugar. (Even after many years in Britain, this still shocks me.) This time, Andy does not comment on my tea, but introduces his helper: 'My son, Jack!' The young man mutters two or three words, then gets on with his work in his brand-new white trainers.

Tools litter the floor. Drills, cables, hammers, screwdrivers, saws, knives, other bits and bobs. Once they begin to take down my old windows in the main room there is loud banging, drilling, more banging. It is a violent scene to watch. Then the frames are out. My God, an open hole on the wall, with the ocean waves roaring in front of us! I feel unnerved, vulnerable. I pray that nothing goes wrong with the new ones. That Andy and his son fit them properly. Otherwise they must, must, must put back the old ones, fill that big hole back up! I won't survive with this huge hole in my flat.

Andy does not seem to have any concerns. His movements are mechanical and routine, he does what he needs to do while instructing his son in different tasks. As I watch them nervously, he begins a monologue:

'You know, I used to have Polish workers helping me. God, those Poles! You really cannot trust them! To be honest, they're just lazy. And unreliable, and they're never happy. You tell them to come to the site at nine and they'll turn up half an hour later or at a quarter to ten and they're already grumpy when they get in and won't even apologise for the delay. And by the end of the day, they complain and all they want is a drink. You can't really trust their word, those Poles, and those Romanians too. I didn't have to deal with those Romanians but my brother-in-law had a hard time with them. At the end of the day, you wonder why they came to England if they complain all the time. But the Poles have gone back home now and I have my son to help me. If I didn't have a son then I'd have trouble finding workers, trustworthy workers, that is. Jack, take down that bit of wood and hand me the hammer, will you . . .'

He goes on and on. An hour and a half later, the hole is filled with the brand-new frames and windows.

'The first piece usually takes a while to finish, but once that's done the rest will be quick,' Andy assures me. 'What do you think? Better, aren't they?'

I nod, vaguely. Yes, sure, I'd expect them to be better given what I am to pay! Only time will tell if they are better. I put my fingers under the windowpanes where the draught usually flows in. I don't feel any cold air there. Well, good – for now at least. They look firm, modest, simple and functional. I do hope these double-glazed and environmentally unfriendly new windows will serve their purpose. Otherwise I will be furious. And I will have to find the last remaining Polish builders to do the job. And I will have high energy bills to pay.

'And you know the other day they rescued nearly eight hundred migrants from the boat, refugees, that's the proper word. How can we let them in? It's ridiculous those lefty and green people, they even wait there on the coast just to rescue them and pull the boat onto the bank. That's really crazy. Those immigrants, what are they going to do here? I mean, really, shit, where are we going to put them? Better lock your door when you go down for a pint. If it was up to me, if I was the Border Police, I'd shoot them right on the boat. And I have done that actually, with my mates and others when I served in the army in Gibraltar! We shot them, on the sea, really, those Africans! They wouldn't tell you about it, but we did that in Gibraltar . . .'

Jack is shifting uneasily, he keeps interrupting and telling his father to hand him over this and that, until suddenly there is a loud blasting noise from his drill. So Andy's monologue is terminated at the moment I actually find it most interesting. I want to ask Andy about Gibraltar, and his army service. I have heard that many older locals here have served in the army in overseas territories when they were young. But the noise is so loud in the flat that no one can talk or hear anything but the drill. I decide to let them do their work. Better leave them alone. The holes have to be filled. The windows have to be replaced. Regardless of Andy's hatred of foreigners, I have faith in his craftsmanship.

The Wind and the Duke

The aluminium windows have been installed in time. Days are brighter than last month, but the weather is still poor in early May. The wind has grown stronger and stronger throughout the night. The weather forecast announced yesterday: 'A wind and rain advisory is in effect for East Sussex, starting at 1 p.m.' Among other dramatic predictions is the following: 'Large tree branches will sway and move. Some coastal routes, seafronts and coastal communities will be affected by spray and/or large waves.'

In the early hours of the morning, two or three o'clock, the sound of waves wakes me up. Violent howling, but no rain yet. When the pale light rises around six, the wind has become intense. Wind knots will be around 45, reaching 50 knots by evening. That means the wind speed is roughly 100 kilometres an hour. Knots, the measurement for wind speed – what an interesting word for a non-anglophone person. As if a pair of trained eyes saw tangles and whirlpools, like knots, in the flow of the air.

Whatever the number of knots is outside, it is too miserable to venture out today. No wonder my child prefers to stay in London and hang out with her schoolmates. She wouldn't even be able to play on the beach with this storm, and she would miss her school.

Cooking myself oat porridge, I put on a layer of clothing over my pyjamas. I make some tea. Not a single soul is on the seafront, no ships in view, only a red flag flapping wildly on the beach, a warning to bathers. It is bleak.

It was because of this very wind that William, Duke of Normandy, could not set out to sea on the date he originally planned. He had to wait for favourable winds. Wind destroys. Wind uproots. Wind kills. But wind also helps, and fills the sails of the ships and carries them along.

William the Conqueror is also known as William the Bastard, because he was illegitimate. His mother Herleva was one of the mistresses of the Duke of Normandy, Robert I. Herleva was a common girl from a town called Falaise. Even though she was the daughter of a tanner, she had an unusual pride and a sense of nobility. Legend has it that when the duke first espied her, she was wearing a dress, the hem of which she raised slightly to attract him. Enchanted by her beauty he brought a white horse for her. So the common girl passed through the castle gates on this horse as a mark of their unofficial relationship.

Little is known about Herleva's fortunes after the birth of William. I read that she later married and produced more children. I imagine a nine-year-old boy called William jumping up and down on the beach of Normandy – a similar scene to my own child playing on Hastings beach. Caressed by the same wind, the same weather conditions. But William would be messing about along with his local gang of boys. He might not be the biggest or tallest in the group, but perhaps he is the most aggressive one. On the windy beach, he would swing his arms and throw a flattened stone into the sea to compete with his friends, but his eyes have probably already looked out towards the land on the other side. There is a detail I read in the English historian Marc Morris's book *William I* that will never escape me, a detail the *Anglo-Saxon Chronicle* fails to provide. One night in 1051, a 23-year-old William marched with his men to the neighbouring town of Alençon. On arrival at the castle wall he was mocked by gatekeepers, who said that his mother was a tanner's daughter, and he was illegitimate. This provoked the young duke; he immediately took over the castle and killed the thirty-two men in the blink of an eye. He ordered them to be mutilated – their hands and feet were chopped off – and the bodies were hanged by the gate. Such was his aggression and temper that in fear and horror the people of Alençon quickly surrendered. Perhaps this was already presaging his victory over the Anglo-Saxons some years later. He knew about the wind, and the wind knots. Had he not understood the wind, maybe he wouldn't have won the Battle of Hastings, even with his most violent temper. The wind and the duke had to be on the same side of history, at precisely the right moment.

Swanneck

Once a week, sometimes twice a week, I walk towards the West Marina. It is a suburb of Hastings, in West St Leonards. There are beach huts and holiday homes there. A shopping mall and a railway station on the hill. But the area used to be called Bulverhythe Village, an ancient place with a small harbour and pier. In modern times, it is where the remains of the eighteenth-century cargo ship *Amsterdam* can be seen. The *Amsterdam* was a legendary ship owned by the Dutch East India Company. In 1749 it sailed for Batavia (now Jakarta) but was almost immediately wrecked on the water in Hastings. I have never seen the cargo remains; I am not hugely interested in shipwrecks. My destination is always the West Marina Gardens by the water. I go here to wander around the meadow with its statues of Harold and Edith. I know the statues and the garden so well now. I see the plants growing and withering. Each time, new flowers have just bloomed while others have died. A few fresh roses are being planted around the double statue. A small board with the words 'Edith's Garden', handwritten with a paintbrush, hangs by the gate, so small that it sways in the wind. One can tell that this is a community garden, run by a group of locals. I like the idea of Edith's Garden, with no mention of King Harold. The newly planted roses are a hopeful message in this otherwise dilapidated area.

Edith Swanneck was also called Edith Swanneschals, or Edith the Fair. Her name in Old English, Ealdgȳð Swann hnesce, meant Edith the Gentle Swan. I rather like her name, though I wonder about why the word 'neck' is in her name. A swan's neck suggests fragility, for sure. She was born around 1025. Her parents were among the richest landowners in England at the time of the Norman Conquest. Some believe she died in the year of the battle. Others believe she lived for two more decades. I cannot find much information on how she died. Harold's body was horribly mutilated by the Norman army, and the Norman army refused to surrender it for burial, despite pleas to William by Harold's mother. According to folklore, it was then that Edith Swanneck walked through the carnage of the battle so that she might identify Harold by markings on his chest known only to her. But much of this is a myth, a sentimental and sorrowful account of the demise of the last Anglo-Saxon king.

After the battle, Edith disappears from the historical record. She may have lived out her life in a nunnery. Some records claim she and her daughter found their way by boat to Denmark, and from there they went to Kiev. At least some historians believe that Edith's daughter Gytha married a prince in Kiev and became a princess of Kievan Rus. Here again, Haestingas, back and forth, a tribe of nowhere and everywhere.

Of course, the whereabouts of Edith Swanneck's deathbed would not cause any disturbance to anyone. She belonged to the defeated. On the night of her death, too, a comet might have passed in a distant sky, somewhere in ancient Burma or bustling Constantinople. No one would notice anything unusual. Certainly not those busy working monks who were noting down the great events for the *Anglo-Saxon Chronicle*. Their candlelight was faint, and the night cold. Men can only live for so long.

Grey Hair

One of the films I watched soon after coming to Britain was *The Lion in Winter*. It is a 1968 film based on a play by James Goldman. I was keen to understand British history – at least, I told myself that I should have some basic knowledge about a few key figures. The film is about the power struggle within the royal family, between Henry II of England (Peter O'Toole) and his wife Eleanor of Aquitaine (Katharine Hepburn). I wanted to see how the family tree of William the Conqueror had sprouted, and what it had produced. Henry II was the great-grandson of the conqueror; his mother, Queen Matilda, was the daughter of Henry I, the youngest son of William I. Even combing through that bit of family tree is exhausting. My hair has grown grey. I will name each strand of my grey hair Henry or William. It's insufferable – everyone in the family bears the same name, everyone is married to a member of the same clan. The unhealthy genes seem to have spread and promoted the unhealthy ruling class mentality.

The Lion in Winter appears to tell a stereotypical narrative about royal families – rival brothers trying to kill each other in order to inherit power from the father king. But what I like most is the woman character in this macho narrative – the imprisoned Eleanor of Aquitaine. She was once the French queen, but she divorced her husband King Louis VII then married her cousin King Henry and became the English queen. She was probably the wealthiest and most powerful woman in Western Europe during that time. But even with all that fortune, she did not have much of a life. She ended up being imprisoned by her husband, which in those days a king husband could do if he didn't like his queen wife, rather than simply chopping off her head. The plot is one of the most dramatic narratives an actor or actress could dream of playing. And of course that's a perfect fit for Katharine Hepburn, a perfect queen of Hollywood cinema. The film makes me think of marriage among nobility, where love and affection are the least of their considerations, where marriage is a means for grasping yet more power and wealth. In a sense, this sort of marriage is always doomed, as soon as one side of the power alliance loses ground.

When I came to Hastings, and when I saw the statue of the dying Harold, held by Edith Swanneck, I wanted to imagine for myself how the domestic life between Harold and Edith played out, or indeed if there was any domestic life between them at all, especially since Edith spent part of her lifetime in a nunnery, as well as hiding in Normandy while Harold struggled to solidify his power. How many servants and slaves did they have in their castle? What did they eat, how did they wash themselves, these last Anglo-Saxons? The arrangements of ancient kitchens, or the rituals of their bathing and defecating, may not be that important, but I am genuinely interested in a civilisation one thousand years ago, which took place where I live now. I am standing on the same land that was once witness to such a narrative. I am a foreigner turned local. Well, not really a local. But perhaps I might become one, if I stick around in this new postcode for the rest of my life – until my hair goes completely grey.

3
Summer

Trampling on Books

There is a detail in Rubens' painting *The Consequences of War*, which I didn't notice at first. As Mars the god of war advances towards those terrified naked bodies, his heavy-sandalled foot tramples an open book. What kind of book is that? Next to the book, there is also a drawing. Why is there a book, a single book, under his foot in such a dramatic painting? What kind of book? Bible? Peace Treaty of Thirty Years War? And what drawing is it?

My eyes cannot find any detail in a reproduction of such an old painting. But perhaps the idea is clear: during the war, arts and books are destroyed and burned in the chaos.

Many emperors and dictators have burned books. One of the most noted book-burning years was 1933, in Nazi Germany. Forty thousand people gathered to hear a speech by the propaganda minister Joseph Goebbels to denounce cultural products with 'un-German spirit'. Apparently, the crowds cheered with enthusiasm and watched the burning of books. These burned volumes included works by Marx, Brecht, Einstein, Freud, Kafka, Thomas Mann, Victor Hugo. Among the flamed pages was also the work of the nineteenth-century Jewish poet Heinrich Heine, who wrote: 'where they burn books, they will in the end burn human beings too'.

Is it ironic (or rational) that the god of war is married to the god of love? Mars and Venus are the unity of war and peace. The myth says that Venus dominates Mars. But perhaps Rubens' painting has contradicted that myth. In Rubens' lifetime, he witnessed the Thirty Years War within the Holy Roman Empire, and as a result he painted Venus as a secondary force in his painting. She tries to restrain Mars. Her arm reaches out ineffectually, a gesture of pain and angst. Her pale and voluptuous naked body is ready to make the sacrifice for peace. But she does not manage to stop the horror. In the painting, her husband is terrorising mothers and children, who are lying on the ground. Those vulnerable bare limbs appear as powerless as the destroyed book and unknown drawing beneath the feet of Mars.

Trampling on books. Strangely, many old books manage to survive regardless of their fate in war.

Here in my Hastings flat, I keep very few books. Two novels by Virginia Woolf. One by Robert Louis Stevenson. They seem to be appropriate books to have here. Then there is my heavy copy of the Domesday Book, and the *Anglo-Saxon Chronicle*. Both are on my bedside table. But not much more. In the bathroom I keep a copy of Dickens's *Bleak House*. That's it. In this flat, I simply do not want to live among books like I always did in the past. Here, nature is the real book I should pay attention to. And I have fields and hills and beaches to walk on. The idea of trampling on books is less drastic for me here, though I am not less entangled with the idea of learning and gaining knowledge in my everyday life. Especially knowledge about Hastings, about Europe, about its past.

But how can one dwell simultaneously on reflections of grand history and the trivia of domestic life? Maybe some men can. Nietzsche could. William Wordsworth could. But me, I cannot. I have to put down the books now. I have an urgent task. I have just discovered some mould growing on the new sealant I have put under the window frames. A line of dark, sticky mould. Disturbing. I have to deal with this. Mould means water ingress on my wall and in my new window frames, and I will have trouble when the next storm comes. That also means I will have to find a builder again to either replace my windows or repair the walls. Whichever way, it will consume money, time and energy.

Jubilee

Hundreds, thousands of British flags flutter above local pubs and bars. I hear there are even extended bank holidays. I used to be unfamiliar with bank holidays as a Chinese person. The face of Queen Elizabeth stares out from every charity-shop window. (But why in charity shops, the dingiest stores of every English high street? Perhaps the Queen and charity shops have some secret affinity that a foreigner like me has no insight into at all?)

Newspapers lying around on the cement by a fish and chips shop carry the headline: 70 YEARS ON THRONE. I read a second headline from the *Sun*: WE LOVE YOU MA'AM. Another one: DON'T YOU JUST LOVE E-II-R? I pick up the oil-stained newspaper from the ground. The Queen seems to have had exactly the same expression all her life, just look at pictures when she was young compared to now. She is ninety-six this year. Reflects well on the hard-working National Health Service? But I do not notice her thanking the NHS on this important day.

I switch on the radio. The eleven o'clock news on the BBC goes out in this order:

> *Crowds descended on the Mall to celebrate the Queen's Plat-*
> *inum Jubilee, which marks its celebration with a four-day bank*
> *holiday.*
> *Millions of households in the UK suffer from food poverty.*

Food banks are being set up currently to help 2 million children in need of food.

Hollywood star Johnny Depp wins his court battle with ex-wife Amber Heard. He will play a gig in Gateshead in England as his first public appearance since the verdict.

Can this really be the order of the news, for today? The order of things, what goes first, what comes second, must have been carefully considered. And 2 million hungry children in the Queen's own country is deemed not so important, it cannot compete with the news about the Queen herself. The war in Europe is not even mentioned. Has the war in Ukraine ended today? Has even Putin decided to take a holiday during the Queen's party time? The issue of mass poverty in this First World country merits only a brief mention alongside news of Johnny Depp's lawsuit? I have not checked the budget for the Queen's Jubilee celebration, nor the Johnny Depp trial costs. Call me naive, but perhaps just one day's cost from either of these events would feed a few million.

But as a foreigner, I don't mind learning that the Queen has been on her throne for seventy years, the longest-serving British monarch. Indeed, as the BBC radio never stops repeating: what a remarkable woman, what an impressive personality! Though how much of an ordeal she has had to endure on a daily basis I would not know. For example, she must have had to observe protocols for every hour she has lived in her life. She would not be able to go to the toilet during her multiple audiences, even if she might experience an urgent need, and she would have to suppress her burps during state banquets. Surely a British diet would make her break wind frequently and she would have to repress her emissions on many occasions. Maybe I'm being naive again. Would the Queen feel her daily life is a tedious ordeal, given that she has never known anything else? We must try to imagine ourselves in other people's shoes. But can we imagine the Queen's life, in the shoes of the

Queen? And what kind of shoes does she wear, in order for us to imagine? They won't be from my home town in China, a major hub for the shoe-making industry, which then exports the shoes overseas.

At the conclusion of the radio news, the presenter interviews a group of women watching the parade for the Jubilee. Some are from America: Ohio and Minnesota. One of the women speaks in a very rounded accent. She says enthusiastically:

'I am so excited to be celebrating the Jubilee! I came all the way from the United States and I just love the Queen!'

To this, the presenter responds:

'But as far as I am aware, your country is not under the Queen's rule. I think you managed to become independent from Britain, way back, in 1776!'

I smile. So the BBC is the state voice, but not every BBC presenter voices state propaganda. Here the dry and subtle British humour works, even for someone like me.

The Flypast

After a day of being drowned in street parties, festooned with thousands of British flags, I was determined to pay some attention to this sort of state celebration, in order to be a good immigrant, an involved subject. So when I see the beacon in the East Hill of Hastings lit up at night (the first time I have seen the beacon on the hill lit), and when I see on the TV in the pub the white smoke trailing fighter jets in a rarely blue English sky, I seek out more information. This is what I read from the Royal Air Force official website (raf. mod.uk):

> *The Royal Navy, British Army and Royal Air Force celebrated Her Majesty the Queen's Platinum Jubilee today with Trooping the Colour and a spectacular flypast in London.*

Then I read the complete order of the flypast, with innumerable aircraft. The list of aircraft is incredible, most bearing the names of animals. Just like the Queen herself, the Royal Air Force loves animals. Wildcat, puma, merlin, hawk, all these carnivorous creatures. And check this out: fifteen Typhoon aircraft. What are they? I study the website. It explains that the Typhoon is a type of precision-combat aircraft, highly capable for multiple purposes such as ground attacks and close air fighting. It has been used at the Falkland Island airbase as well as in the Black Sea region. The picture of the Typhoon does not say much to a hopeless non-military person like me. It just looks like any other military jet I have seen in a film. At least I can recognise the 'Hawk' of the Red Arrows, because of its striking red-coloured body and a British flag painted on its tail.

So I have learned that more than seventy aircraft from the Royal Services are doing their jobs for the celebration. Spectacle in place of history? The flypast will go over Buckingham Palace, while the royal family watches 'from the famous balcony'. No one can be bothered to explain to a foreigner like me what this 'famous balcony' is, but I imagine it to be like the balcony where Chairman Mao and Premier Zhou Enlai stood along with Communist generals on Tiananmen Square in Beijing, waving to the workers, soldiers and proletarians of the country. That was in 1949. There was no royal family around. The last emperor, Puyi, after spending time in a war prison, was remodelled as an ordinary citizen and was made to join the Communist Party a few years later. He worked as a gardener, not in a royal garden, but a people's park in Shanghai, to be exact.

Tostig, Tosti, Tosi, Who Cares

The year 1066 has one of the longest entries in the *Anglo-Saxon Chronicle*. It includes the description of a comet when Harold Godwinson came onto the political scene, as though this might compensate for not mentioning the birth of Harold in the entry for 1022. The entry is also written in an unusual style. It reads very much like narrative prose. I wonder how much of it was added, revised and beautified later on, years after the Norman Conquest.

> A.D. 1066. *This year came King Harold from York to Westminster, on the Easter succeeding the midwinter when the king (Edward) died. Easter was then on the sixteenth day before the calends of May. Then was over all England such a token seen as no man ever saw before. Some men said that it was the comet-star, which others denominate the long-hair'd star. It appeared first on the eve called 'Litania major', that is, on the eighth before the calends off May; and so shone all the week.*

The comet shone all the week! It must have been perplexing for medieval people to take in. A comet is a gassing thing, originally an icy-cold matter in the solar system, but while passing the sun it warms up and begins to release gas, then humans see its white trail in the dark sky. Cold and hot in one body, through time and space. What did the monks then see in a passing comet? A dramatic statement of the arrival of a historical figure? Or an omen of a disastrous event that one would not dare to verbalise in fear of its imminent consequence?

There is a passage about King Harold and his brother Tostig's power struggle written in such a theatrical form that it creates suspense leading to the main events. The chroniclers paid careful attention to Tostig – also known as Tosty, Tosti and Tosi, but who cares about the exact spelling of his name? He was merely the brother of the king, who eventually slew him, like so many others slew so many others.

But Tostig was lucky (if only for a short while). Apparently the King of the Scots entertained him, and aided him with supplies. The spoiled Tostig lived under the protection of the Scots that summer, and there, he met the King of Norway. In the chronicle it was recorded that the Norwegian king arrived with three hundred ships. Knowing that those northern kings would be the supporters of his immense ego, Tostig entered into an alliance with him, and the two ganged up against Harold.

Reading about the power struggle between Tostig and his brother king tires me out. It reminds me of my school years in China, when we were made to learn the names of all the sons of the emperors, and there were so many emperors in a dynasty! And we have so many dynasties in Chinese history! That's why I hated history at school. History is unbearable for a young person. But here and now, I am a foreign woman living in the West who bears no local history. I do feel this unbearable lightness of being when sitting alone in a crowded pub or a cafe full of chatty local families. Perhaps by reading the footnotes of British history, I might be able to enter the Western world, perhaps even with some insight in a way that other migrants do not. I tell myself that my obsession with the Anglo-Saxon reality and its past is perhaps one of the key elements to understanding the current world order, a white Anglo-Saxon-centred world.

The Justice and Legality of War

To me, all wars are immoral. All wars are wrong. Yet, some wars seem less wrong than others. If one state or country or group attacks another, then surely the latter has a right to respond, to fight back. Their action is justified, at least in some cases. Thomas Aquinas, a thirteenth-century Italian philosopher, theologian and priest, thought there was just war and unjust war. The kingdoms of medieval Europe were deeply concerned with this distinction, even if it could be used as propaganda to justify actions regarding their peoples or other states. There is clearly a minefield of issues here, which I don't know how to walk through. But I can recognise some unjust wars.

Take the Opium Wars which occurred in the mid nineteenth century between Britain and China. These wars were triggered by the Chinese government's campaign to enforce its prohibition against opium trafficking by British merchants. We know that the Chinese military leader Lin Zexu sent Queen Victoria a letter about the negative effects of trading opium on the people of China. But apparently the British queen never received the letter. When the Chinese acted to stop the trade by burning opium, the Royal Navy surrounded the Canton area and bombarded the Chinese ships and harbour. Britain's superior military forces defeated the Chinese. As a result they forced China to sign unequal treaties to grant favourable trade concessions, reparations and territory to Western powers, which led to China's 'century of humiliation'. Hong Kong was one of the ports that were handed over to the British Empire. In the West, there is no general opinion that these wars were immoral, unjust or even illegal. It seems that justice is a one-way street. The justice of the victors. The question of just and unjust wars makes me think of Putin's invasion of Ukraine. For us it is unjust, for Putin it is just. For Putin, his war, or special military operation, is morally right because it is required for national survival.

Would Putin's war have been morally acceptable if he had openly declared his intention of carrying out a military operation in Ukraine? No. Putin's invasion is no better or worse than the US–UK coalition invasion of Iraq. Both gave justifications. The coalition lied about weapons of mass destruction. Putin lied about the need to remove the fascists from Ukraine. It's the same old story. What about 1066? William, Duke of Normandy, claimed that he was the rightful heir to the throne, and that Harold was the illegal usurper, and that Harold had in fact promised him the throne. And so on and so forth. Even if true, does it justify what followed? Obviously not. Reality does not matter, as usual. What mattered was that men were moved by William, by his talk or by the threat of his violence, or both. Right belongs with might. It's the greatest cliché, but it proves itself again and again. If you have no weapons, then moralise as you will, it makes no difference. The duke was lucky. The tide of the sea and the tide of human affairs just happened to go his way. That's the reality of justice.

Classification of Refugees

In a local pub, the TV is on. Though no one is actually watching as it's not showing a football match. A BBC news channel is showing a debate in the House of Lords. There are hundreds of old men in a hall, mostly white-haired. I suppose they are all Lords, who are unelected. How feudal, I can't help but feel that way. British politics seems impossible for outsiders to understand. The prime minister has tried to pass a bill classifying refugees, basically to punish the refugees branded as 'illegal', those who enter the county via the most dangerous routes, even if there is no such thing as an 'illegal' refugee under international law. Listening to the debate, I learn that refugees who made their own way to Britain (rather than through complicated Home Office schemes) would be given an inferior form of protection with limited rights. That means anyone arriving by a small boat across the Channel could have their claim ruled as inadmissible and receive a jail sentence of up to four years. And on top of that, they won't receive any public funds, and could have their family members barred from joining them.

Such a cruel policy – how could any politician in a democratic country try to pass it without any shame? Or am I being naive again? And surely this won't stop the desperate from trying to cross the Channel water. Some will drown in the grey blue, some will survive but may end up in jail, and some will be sent back. If only the British government had used the same measure to deal with the

Channel crossing a thousand years ago to stop the Normans' invasion. Then there would never have been a Battle of Hastings, and there would never have been generations of French chevaliers stealing English lands, and there would never have been the creation of the Domesday Book commissioned by William the Conqueror in order to tax the English in the most thorough way, thus creating a new class system which seems to have become the everlasting social structure of the English society.

Flood

The rains are relentless. The wind persists. Nature's force exceeds far beyond the force of tribal warfare. In an inland city such as London or Leeds or Nottingham, storms only bring heavy rains, lasting a day or two, causing some leaking for a few unfortunate old dwellings. But here in Hastings, a proper storm is a tempest. Yes, tempest is a great word, partly due to Shakespeare. But even without mentioning Shakespeare it is still a word that has the power to stun foreigners or non-Anglo-Saxons. At least it stuns someone like me.

There are detailed records of floods in this area. As you move around the coast, you can see the different watermarks on the piers and water breaks along the beaches. There are red warning marks on the barriers along the promenade. I found some records on the website of the local council. The Grand Parade area around St Leonards where I live has been flooded repeatedly. The primary cause of each flood is noted, 'storm at high tide', or 'water rise by a blocked road gutter', and so on. One entry in particular seems to capture the effect of water in a coastal town: 'Waves came over the wall, drains blocked by shingles, basement and first floor flooded.' This incident occurred at Harold Place Underpass. (Harold Place? Does that name refer to King Harold Godwinson? Or is it just some rich Harold from the last century?)

Finally I found a record of my building. The last flooding was six years ago: 'Wind blown spray and shingle from waves hitting vertical sea wall in area of shingle erosion flooding the basement.' The sentence is long, the grammar slightly confusing for me. Is it clear for others? I have never entered the basement of my building, which is always locked. I imagine rats swimming in the black water down there, the stench of rotting things trying to escape the entrapment. I won't imagine more.

The more I read these records, the more there is to fear. Especially now, as I sit inside with a rainstorm by my window, raindrops splattering the panes. The windowsills vibrate, so do the walls. Outside, the sea is in a rage. Waves are rushing in and upward and then out and downward in a constant fury. Even with the windows tightly shut, I still hear the sound of the waves crashing. The back of my flat, which faces the hills and the Old Town, does not suffer any less abuse from the gales. If I was a spirit hovering above the chimneys of my building, I would be able to see the elements battering it from all sides, the damning swirls like a great moving matrix.

The temperature drops. The windowsills inside are now wet. Not quite dripping, but water has seeped in, gathering in a little pool on the surface. What is happening to my brand-new aluminium windows? Andy promised the new frames and double-glazed glass would prevent the damp and draught! In his words 'They will last fifty years!' Liars. Builders are all the same. I curse. But maybe it was a scam from the beginning when I met Andy in the paint shop. He wanted quick cash and he wanted his window-seller mates to have orders from a foreigner and an idiot like me.

I grab a towel and start to wipe the wet surface along the windowsills. I think of a biblical story about rain that falls for forty days and forty nights. It rains until the highest mountains in the world are covered, and all earth-based life perishes except for Noah and the animals because they are saved in the Ark.

What would it be like, if we had to live through forty days of rain? Britain has not had that record. Nowhere on this planet has. Not yet. I check the total rainy days in England per year. The number fluctuates. But last year there were approximately 171 days in which 1mm or more of rain fell. The year before it was 168 days. This year, I don't know. Surely the numbers would be higher if I look up Wales or Scotland. I prefer not to. It would be depressing. It's absurd to think that England is the driest country in the UK, even though it is.

I watch the rain by the window and keep mopping the wet sills inside. I notice the mouldy sealant is breaking apart under the window frames. Already! I touch the sealant patch. It feels spongy. More rain will seep in. I need to run to buy some sealant now.

Wild Garlic

On the hills around Fairlight, and all the way to the Kent coast, giant ferns grow everywhere. But there are countless other wonders in this wildness. My walks on those hills are distracted and unhurried, mainly because I pause when my eye is caught by a familiar or unfamiliar plant, some blossoming so wonderfully that I have to stop, stay still, and admire them for a while. Often, I encounter a colony of gold-yellow sunflowers, their expression so joyful and happy. Or I pass close by long-stemmed purple wolfsbane (though I call them wolf's gloves). I love their wicked shapes. There are white clusters of anemones. Sometimes I stumble upon a red Irish saxi-frage bush, nestled within the jungle of ash trees and pines. Their flowers are discreet and small, but firm and tough. I bend down to study their petals, or touch their strange-shaped leaves.

But I rarely pick the flowers. Except for wild garlic. Whenever I pass through a wet part of the woodland, in almost any season, the distinct odour of wild garlic catches my attention. I lower my head to look for the long green blades. They grow in dense patches, their white flowers dangling down. If I am on the way back home, I pluck some and put them in my bag. And my heart will be content know-ing I'll have some organic vegetables to cook this evening, even though I am still a long way from home, even though I know the soil in which this young garlic grows was once drenched in blood from the Norman soldiers and the locals.

I eat garlic leaves as I would eat lettuce. I could eat them every day. I fry them with oil and salt, or I chop them up and add to noodles. Their sweet and spicy flavour is so hearty that they ground my day. They are my happy leaves. Heaven knows how many garlic leaves I ate with my family when I lived in China. We grew different types of onions in our backyard: chives, scallions, leeks, garlic. With their strong scent, no rabbits or birds wanted to touch them. So we would eat their leaves in the spring and harvest their bulbs in the autumn.

I read that in ancient times, Egyptian slaves were given a daily ration of garlic to ward off illness and to increase their physical strength. When the slaves threatened to stop building the pyramids, their ration of garlic was increased by their masters. This makes me think of the ruined Hastings Castle. Over the last thousand years, the castle has, multiple times, fallen into disrepair, and periodically been rebuilt, only to collapse again. Even today, the local council wants to regenerate it, to rebuild the part that has tumbled into the sea. For now, nothing is being done. More garlic? Or some garlic

spirit? Something must be missing in the natural environment around that castle. A feng shui master might say: in order to re-erect the castle, you have to erect a garlic goddess opposite the castle. Thus the violent wind can travel in a more friendly way, and the two edifices can protect and benefit one another.

So I do a lot of wild-garlic walks in the countryside. Sometimes my walk will lead me from East Sussex towards Kent. I am not sure if I ever cross the invisible border between the two shires. Hikers look at the maps during their walks, I look at the plants to tell if I am on the right path.

One weekend, when Moon and her father were visiting, I cooked some garlic leaves for them, but they refused to touch the dish. I watched them chew their rice, drenched in soy sauce. I tried to convince them, but they wouldn't go near the wild leaves. Perhaps it's because they once witnessed how I got poisoned by eating supposed wild garlic – I mistook some crocuses for my holy leaves. Crocuses can be lethal and I could have died. Still, it won't stop me from foraging.

July

It is 7 July 2022. Boris Johnson has just resigned as prime minister. No one in Britain seems to be surprised, apart from me. I thought he would manage to stay in his position at least to the end of his term, as he had already managed to avoid all punishment so many times. He could have joked away about his previous mistakes and then moved on to the next, but apparently fifty ministers resigned in advance of his own resignation. In China, this sort of event would form a new revolution, as bloody as Mao brought about in 1949. But here no one has died and Johnson even made a sensible resignation speech. I took the time to listen to his jabber. One line caught my ear: 'Being a prime minister is an education in itself.' Yes, he meant it. But who else could have such an education at the cost of 67 million people's livelihoods? Another startling line: 'When the herd moves, it moves.' Finally, I saw the pictures of him hugging and kissing his wife and his child. Almost certainly he wants to appear to be an obedient husband, even if he is not an obedient student.

There has been a heatwave all week. The temperature rises to 30 degrees, which is unusual for Britain. Everyone is complaining, but I am loving it. The sea and the beach are perfect in this temperature. Meanwhile, the new leadership contest is heating up too. I have paid some vague attention to it, though my eyes are mostly fixed on the beach and the blue water.

Tides

Since the beginning of the summer, I have developed a daily habit of reading the details of the tides along the coast here. I try to understand the tides, in a technical way. Even though the locals have told me that there is nothing to 'understand'. Tides are just tides. It's the pull of the moon and the sun. But the pull of the moon and the sun is the whole cosmos, surely it is very complex. Also the coastline of Britain has changed in the last thousand years, but have the tides changed with it? I wish I had a god's-eye view on the changes of history! In my everyday life, apart from spending time endlessly gazing at the waves from my window, I pay great attention to the exact measurement in metres of the high and low tides.

This morning, I read that the next low tide will be in 6 hours and 24 minutes. The next high tide will be in 11 hours and 46 minutes. I am fascinated by such precise predictions: the tide will be 0.71 metres during its lowest, and 7.54 metres at its highest. I raise my head and look at the sea through my window, I see neither metres nor tidal timing but the vast splash of angry waves. Science makes me feel rather stupid, and nature makes me feel powerless. When I look at a chart as such, it makes me feel the weightlessness of my occupations. I am just someone engaged in poetic nonsense, really, I am a drifting non-entity. And this feeling is only confirmed, even reinforced, when I walk outside to look at the changing clouds, the whirling seagulls, and to feel the water-drenched shingles under my feet.

Orchard and Sewage

Reading the *Hastings Independent* makes me more 'local', as well as 'aged' in a good way. In a cafe or a pub, I can see that only middle-aged people read local papers these days, as younger people read the news on their smartphones.

Today I read that a local community proposes to plant 'up to 20 fruit trees' on the westernmost of the West Hill lawns. What a good idea, I think. I know that place, there's a great view above the ocean but it is slightly bare with just grass and bushes. Cherries and apples would add so much to the walk on the hills. They also aim to plant 'up to 39 trees' on the lower half of Bembrook Open Space, an inland area towards the town of Ore. I am interested in these measured words: 'up to 39 trees'. From a Chinese perspective, it is not common to encounter such a way of going about things. In China, the 'normal' way would be to plant as much as capacity allows; because the land is vast and the population huge, a few fruit trees wouldn't have much of an effect. Here in England, it feels like things have to be carefully measured. As I read more, I understand that the trees will be planted eight to ten metres apart. That will form open, outspread orchards with plenty of room for grass and flowers between them. Simple things in England like this have always impressed me, I must admit.

On the next page, I read about the pollution in the sea. A 'local' company, Southern Water, has been infamously pouring sewage water into the coast. Illegal discharges are flowing into the rivers and seas all around this area. As a result, the water in Sussex, Essex, Kent and Hampshire is heavily polluted. Later I read the BBC website, and it reports that even the French are getting angry. They officially appeal to the EU over UK discharge waste into the Channel. The other day, a swimmer on the beach introduced me to an app called Swim Against Sewage. It is an interactive map that records the daily measurement of water pollution in areas along the coast. I thanked him but I am yet to use it. I love the idea that swimmers and surfers interact with the sea even though the water is heavily polluted. I also love the concept of planting fruit trees eight to ten metres apart. We know there is always an evil force somewhere. But then there is also an anti-evil force. Humans are creative in both ways.

Digging

You can tell whether a place is wealthy or poor by looking at the litter in the neighbourhood. The streets around my building are full of rubbish. Pizza boxes (mostly from Domino's delivery), plastic bags (with Tesco branding), crisp packets, broken household items, old mattresses, building materials ... The streets are a dumping yard, a favourite spot for chip-loving seagulls (no wonder bird flu is seriously bad in this area). As I walk, my eyes are caught by oily extractor fans on the wall, rusty diesel cars on the pavement. No trees. No flowers. Not even a glimpse of ivy.

Sometimes I wonder if I should write to the council to complain. Other people might complain about a certain issue once a month, for some years, until they get back a three-line answer. 'Thank you for your letter dated xxx. I am sorry to hear about the condition of your street ...' But even if the council bothers to answer, it will tell me that the streets by the shore aren't suitable for digging. Of course I see the builders digging around here all the time, pipelines, electrical systems, broadband cables. But it's not good for trees, they will say, trees have roots, and roots are bad, they can spread.

I wish I could borrow or buy a spade, so that I could dig and plant trees in my street at night. A guerrilla gardener. But I am sure CCTV is in operation, and I would be found out the next day. Some bureaucrat from the local authority would come down and pull out the young oak or maple I'd have planted. And then the ugly holes on the ground would remain, the council wouldn't even bother to fill them in. The holes would stay, like a rabbit digging out roots in the spring.

I think of Seamus Heaney's 'Digging', a poem he wrote in the sixties before he became well known. I remember the lines about watching his father digging a potato patch with a spade. So good, he wrote, the way his father used a spade, just like his old man. The smell of potato mould, the soggy peat, the turf. All that is behind him but has not left him. As an adult, he possessed a pen, not a spade. This rings true, here and now, in my case, in my part of England. I would like to have a spade, but even if I had a spade, I have no soil to dig. No potato patch. Let alone a flower bed. I have a pen. No, not a pen. A computer. A laptop. That's my spade, for digging, in Hastings.

Meanwhile in the East

In the tenth or eleventh century, when anonymous churchmen, with quills made from the feathers of the left wing of a goose, noted down these events, did they have any notion of what was happening on the other side of the world, in Persia, or Mongolia? The left wing of a goose is not an important detail, but I thought about it sometimes. I learned that in medieval times the right-handed person would use a feather from the animal's left wing because of its perfect curve for the right hand. Or maybe one of the monks wrote in his left hand, and he would be using a feather pen from the right side of the wing of a goose. Either way, they must have had to sharpen the tip of the feather in order to have a thin writing nib. Now I must not let feathers or wings distract my thoughts. I was talking about the other side of the world, wasn't I? One or two bearded old monks may have heard of remote places, such as Persia or Mongolia, but surely they were too preoccupied with their scribal duties and their prayers to let their thoughts wander beyond the Saxon land. Perhaps somewhere in the depths of a Wessex forest, a coughing and ale-loving priest might have obtained a crumpled and stained map on which the supposed world was sketched and primitively coloured. And on that sheepskin map might have been some inky letters indicating where the borders of the Northern or Southern Song Dynasty were imagined to be. Indeed, by 1066, in the Far East, the Northern Song Dynasty had reached the highest degree of civilisation in China's imperial history. Hundreds and thousands of poets, painters and calligraphers as well as martial artists lived out their lives under the eastern sun, unaware of the struggles of a certain Wessex king or a Norman queen. Around the time of the Battle of Hastings, as the old Song Emperor Rengzong was breathing his last breath, his son Shengzong was putting on his heavy golden dragon robes, waiting to be crowned as soon as his father's last gasp entered the heavenly air. The events of this dynasty were abundantly recorded by Chinese courtesans and historians, as well as poets and Taoists, though I wonder if anyone outside the imperial court would have had any access to them. To read them in all their lavish detail would feel like being drowned in history.

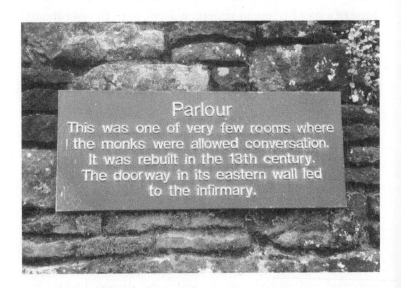

The Chinese Chronicle

Nameless chroniclers. Named historians. Is it possible that named historians present the history in a more subjective way than anonymous ones? During the time of King Harold's death and William's conquest, the Song Emperor Shenzong was at the height of his reign, even though, to the west of the empire, China was at war with the nomads. The Mongols were coming. Mass destruction was on the way. But not quite yet. Sima Guang, supposedly a great imperial minister, spent his entire life noting down the major events of the preceding millennia, volume after volume. It was said the original manuscript amounted to about three hundred scrolls. I wonder how long each scroll would have been. And whether he wrote on bamboo sheets or paper. Paper printing technology was already used in his time. His account of Chinese history, the *Zizhi Tongjian*, translated as *A Comprehensive History of Government*, chronicles events from the Zhou Dynasty to the Song Dynasty. It covers 1,400 years and sixteen dynasties. So vast that hardly any Chinese person has read a tenth of it, even though there are more than a billion people in the country. And no wonder I take the easier case – the Anglo-Saxon one. I might have chosen an American chronicle, for my readings, if I did not live in Hastings.

There are many stories about Sima Guang. A devoted historian, he rejected the reforms to the imperial court promoted by other ministers. In the end he refused further appointment by the emperor even though the court gave him a large number of assistants and granted him full access to the historical archives. He withdrew from the court and public life. I've often wondered why. Did he not want to write an official account of history under the emperor's influence? He might have been the kind of historian who liked to have his own view on historical events and figures. In order to have his own view heard and written down, he had to leave the imperial court. Otherwise his head would be chopped off. In 1071, at the age of fifty-two, Sima Guang took up residence in a town called Luoyang, a place known for its abundance of peony flowers. He lived there as an ordinary man, continuing the compilation of his books. His self-imposed retirement, or rather exile, proved essential for him to finish his vast chronicles, the *Zizhi Tongjian*. One memorable story from his later years is about his pillow. He had a wooden pillow made from a log, designed to slip from under his head whenever he rolled over. He did not want to sleep too much, so that he could have more time to work on his volumes. Each time his head slipped from the log pillow, he would get up and work. He called his pillow Jingzhen, Alert Pillow. Or a more liberal translation: the Pillow of Awareness.

Sima Guang died a year after he submitted to the emperor the complete *Zizhi Tongjian*; he was sixty-six.

Locations

How certain can we be of the exact location of a historical event? The Battle of Hastings is said by some accounts to have taken place on a certain hill and by other accounts to have taken place in a field, some miles away from the hill. Does it matter where precisely the battle took place? It depends on what one is interested in. Archaeologists want to know where precisely. But for people like me who want to know about the impacts of war on the people, it does not matter.

The received view, in the tourist brochures and the modern mythology, is that the Battle of Hastings, and the exact spot where King Harold died, occurred on a field that is now part of a town called, unsurprisingly, Battle. Battle is a few miles west of Hastings. A thousand years ago, it was neither a town nor a village: it was an inland extension of Hastings, which in medieval times was a central town in the production of salt. Today, Battle is a ten-minute train ride from Hastings. Since the town is small, anyone who gets to Battle will inevitably walk on Senlac Hill, the supposed battlefield. One can stand on the peaceful green hill and imagine the ancient fighting scenes. No human remains or artefacts have ever been found at Senlac Hill, though, no mass grave where 10,000 men fell, so some historians claim that the fighting took place on a different hill.

Other historians say that due to the acidic soil the remains would have disintegrated to the point of being undetectable, but this seems strange to me. There are recent finds. An ancient skeleton, evidently a soldier, was found in a medieval cemetery. Originally it was thought to be associated with a battle in the thirteenth century, but more recently it has been associated with Hastings. One skeleton? One skeleton among thousands of dead? We found the fossils of Lucy, one of the oldest human apes from 3 million years ago, but we cannot recover the skeletons from a thousand years ago? Why is that? Lucy was found in Ethiopia, not in England. Is it taboo to turn the English earth upside down? It might well be. There is a huge local resistance towards any initiative that would interfere with the sacred landscapes of this part of England. Indeed, if you have walked in the forests in Suffolk, Kent or Sussex, and have appreciated the thick expanses of greenness, you would not want to dig large holes here and there in the fern-covered earth, you would not want to disturb the land.

I read that there had been recent excavations carried out at Battle Abbey, where King Harold is supposed to have been buried. They found some remnants predating the battle, but nothing relating to the period of the conquest. This is truly mysterious. But again, even if we had managed to find a mass grave by now, it would not mean that was exactly where the battle took place. If indeed there is no mass grave to be found, might it be possible that the locals dragged the corpses into the sea, to let nature swallow the defeated? The ocean has the best antibiotics and antiseptics, so there would be no more pestilence or infections.

Some years ago, I visited Battle briefly. I remember I passed a muddy passage on the hillside, which is part of the 1066 Battle Walk. I looked down at the meadows stretching out before me. Dozens of white-and-black cows idling in the fields, hedges and broken branches here and there along the path. The wooden post by the fields read:

These fields were formerly part of Battle Abbey Estate.
Livestock are present in these fields.
Please keep to the public footpath.
Dogs must be kept on a lead at all times.

I took a photo as my record of the place. As I wandered further, two women were walking in front me. They wore rain jackets and hiking boots. I began to talk to them. They said they were hiking all the way to Bexhill. It would take about three or four hours, the red-haired woman told me. I was attracted to the idea of the long walk. I would have liked to walk with them, for at least half of the length. That day my time was not my own, but I joined for a while, following behind. They chatted about their families as they trudged in the mud. I grasped that the red-haired woman was a local, the other was from Yorkshire. That's a long way from here, if you consider the distance from within England. Passing a dark wood, when the next turn appeared, I said goodbye to them and slowed my pace. I turned back. The cows and sheep were still in the same spot in the field, nothing would trouble them, until the final moments arrived.

On that day trip, I walked around Battle's quaint high street. I took a photo of a butcher's shop as the sign was so impressive: *A. Ray 1066 Butchers*. It gave me a false impression that the shop originated from 1066 and it had always been there in the last thousand years. Curious, I went into the shop. Among piles of naked chicken and lamb legs, the latter shedding droplets of blood onto the marble floor, and under the hanging sausages, I noticed another, smaller, sign: *Established Over 35 years*. Well, that's not nothing. Thirty-five years ago, I was still living in a Chinese province, and could hardly read or speak a word of English. Let alone know there is a town called Battle, somewhere on the other side of the world.

It was a cold day. There was nothing more foreign than my presence wandering those narrow winding pavements. I decided that I wouldn't enter the Battle Abbey. Even though the abbey was the

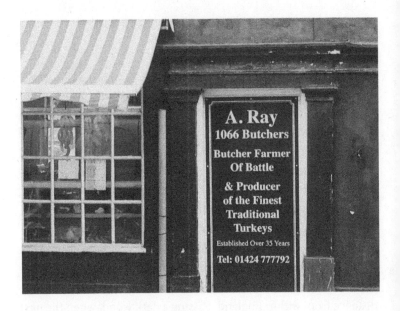

Number One Must See local tourist attraction. You see, I am a half-hearted tourist. In fact, I hate tourism. Such a sad business. Even though I know I am a cultural tourist. My whole existence in the West is some form of cultural tourism, no matter how many years it has been. Right there and then, all I wanted that day was to return to London, a place where I could recognise a few streets and a few faces, which would console me in my dislocated existence.

The Battle for Number 10

August is approaching. My days are filled with uninterrupted summery light. No rain. The beach is more friendly than ever. The shingle banks and sand dunes are warm, even during the early evening. In the twilight, I lie down on the pebble stones, my arms and legs absorbing the heat from the shingles. I want this weather to remain always. Only in this warmth do I feel the friendliness of life, the kindness of nature. Only in this weather do I feel that perhaps I can live here, though 'forever' is a word I shall never use.

But no rain now for weeks means everyone is worrying about drought. It seems unthinkable that this wet place – the British Isles – might run out of fresh water. But then 'reality is scary', as the *Guardian* writes about climate change. The world seems to be an endless mess. In the UK, Parliament is deciding who will be the new prime minister.

Just behind my favourite double statue – the dying King Harold and the weeping Swanneck – is the Marina Fountain Pub. It is a wooden-floored restaurant bar serving Sunday roasts and welcomes kids and dogs. Sometimes, at the end of a long walk, I sit at the bar and read a free copy of the *Hastings Independent*. Today, along with some locals, I watch a TV debate between Rishi Sunak and Liz Truss. I have even ordered a beer, just like a proper English person, a half-pint of Guinness. I have never liked Guinness, but I do not know any other brand names. So I always order the same drink. Which I dislike. As I raise my head to watch a moment in *The Battle for Number 10* on Sky News, I feel that T V debates are the most fraught way for politicians to present their policies, but this format seems to be a norm in the West. Amid the loud noise in the pub, I overhear a conversation between locals.

One says: 'Liz Truss wants the trust of over-sixty-rich-southern-non-urbanites.'

Another: 'But poor rich boy Rishi Sunak is full of bullshit.'

Another: 'Well, if you vote for Rishi, he'll bring over ten thousand of his Indian cousins to West St Leonards!'

And another: 'I don't mind if we have a few more curry restaurants. Chicken masala every night!'

I think about my own judgement on this. I have no preference for either of these politicians, though I have learned that for the Brexit referendum Truss voted Remain and Sunak voted Leave. I also learn that despite their initial differences, both want to 'get Brexit done' as Boris Johnson put it.

In spite of the gloomy politics, the sun shines on in the blue sky. Evening descends with the low tide. The moon is clear and curved, the air clear and sweet. At least here is the real physical sense of warm summer, if only briefly.

The Named and the Unnamed

I must be getting old. Not only do I read the *Anglo-Saxon Chronicle*, I find myself also looking at the Domesday Book. I am interested in that big tome because it was created by the Duke of Normandy after his conquest. I understand that taxation was the reason for compiling such a record. But I want to understand what he cared about immediately after he became the Anglo-Saxon king. Also, the book was written in Old French, as opposed to Old English, which the locals spoke. How did the Normans translate those local names and places, as well as cultures, beyond their lived experiences?

One cannot really look at a random page of the Domesday Book without feeling a slight intrigue. Even for a foreigner, its strange descriptions carry interest if not comprehension. The book is a collection of facts about who owns what. The purpose is for it to enable the ruler to know how much to tax people. The book was written with an authoritative tone, and I wonder where this came from. It must be from the absolute power, given and approved by the conqueror – the Norman King William.

Naturally, I read pages from the section about 'my' shire – Sussex. And I look at the ancient landowners of Hastings around the 1080s. The text reads: *Hastings: Count of Eu and Robert from him.*

Then nothing else is indicated. The survey moves on to the next place and mentions other odd names without any explanation.

Who is him? Wrong translation? Words missing? Did Hastings

change hands to the Normans then, and was the new owner the Count of Eu from Normandy whose name was Robert, the son of William I (not the Conqueror William)? Despite the confusing names, it seems significant that the Count of Normandy was also the Lord of Hastings. He was granted the English land as soon as the Battle of Hastings was won. It was said that this Robert commanded sixty ships in the fleet supporting William's landing in 1066. Only two years after the conquest, Robert was given Hastings Castle, as well as nearby territories previously owned by Viking-Saxons.

The confusion over names must have been a terrible ordeal for the monks who drafted the *Anglo-Saxon Chronicle*, as well as for those who recorded the Domesday Book. A simple example: Robert then produced a son also called William, and William the Conqueror too produced sons with one of them named Robert. I do not understand Western naming habits at all. Couldn't names be slightly different and more creative? If it was for the purpose of reincarnation, I like to think the heavenly mind wouldn't be constrained by any permissible name register. And really, those wildly ambitious men who managed to terrorise half of Europe could not think of a new name other than his own or his father's? Or were the names left to the women in the house, who endured their days waiting for the return of their husbands and sons, though none of them showed up often? In most cases, never.

I think of an old Anglo-Saxon poem called 'The Seafarer' which I stumbled upon in my local library one day. The poem was written in the tenth century in Old English, its author unknown. Supposedly it was written by a man who lived on and by the sea. He talked about his time, before the Norman Conquest, in medieval Britain. I even copied out some lines from the poem in my dairy.

I do not believe
that the riches of the world
will stand forever.

Always and invariably,
one of three things
will turn to uncertainty
before his fated hour:
disease, or old age,
or the sword's hatred
will tear out the life
from those doomed to die.
And so it is for each man
the praise of the living,
of those who speak afterwards,
that is the best epitaph,
that he should work
before he must be gone . . .

I liked the poem immediately on first reading. I thought about how it was something not from an official record such as the chronicle, nor the Domesday Book. It contained the words of an ordinary man who endured hardship. He was not a churchman or an administrator worrying about the official portrait of his lords or local history. He was simply crying out his existence: a life on the sea, by the sea and beyond the sea. I imagine the bearded seafarer sailing his boat through the storm, trying to reach some destination. He knows his wife and children are waiting at home, far from where he is. He does not know if he will ever return. How many have lived, and died, as nameless seafarers, or simply wayfarers? The bulk of lives leave no trace or name. Even those who leave their names in books still perish. Perhaps the only true monument is one's effect on those who live after.

The Route to Canterbury

Though I have been living in East Sussex, close to Kent, I have not yet walked on the famous pilgrim route. The Pilgrims' Way is an ancient track between Winchester and Canterbury, a historical route to Canterbury Cathedral. I have visited towns such as Winchester, Rye and Canterbury, but on different occasions for different purposes. I am not a product of Christianity, but a mix of Confucianism and Buddhism, tinted with my Communist upbringing. Pilgrim paths in Europe do not hold strong attraction for me. But I am curious about what these ancient people saw and felt on their

solitary and weather-beaten walks. I am interested in how they dealt with menacing animals, horrible stormy nights and, ultimately, the ruggedly indifferent seashore landscapes.

But perhaps one doesn't need to go to Canterbury Cathedral to realise the divine existence. I read somewhere that Thomas Becket, later the Archbishop of Canterbury, lived in one of the ancient churches in Hastings. Before Becket was elevated to his fatal position in Canterbury, he was a young man living in this area with wealthy lords as supporters and was a boyhood friend of Henry II, with whom he used to go rambling, hunting and hawking. Henry thought he could rely on Becket to do his bidding, and made him Archbishop of Canterbury in 1162. But Becket had his own mind, and a fight over taxation ensued. Becket ended up dead, stabbed by four thuggish knights, while he knelt in prayer. Christianity is such a feverous religion for us Chinese. It's full of martyrs. Becket saw God, and had become immovable. He could not be swayed by the king. The Christian mind, seems to me, can be so intransigent, so uncompromising. Perhaps this lies in the Christian concept of faith, which we don't really have in Taoist or Confucian practices. I tried to read T. S. Eliot's *Murder in the Cathedral*, which explores this concept of faith. The Becket character's faith is so strong that it leads him to do things that he cannot himself understand. There seems to be no room for compromises. Just absolutes – good and evil.

But perhaps I have been subconsciously avoiding really trying to understand the play. It is laborious enough for a foreigner like me to work out the Battle of Hastings. For me to understand such a play would require so much homework, it would be like going to a re-education camp, run by ecclesiastical Red Guards. Sometimes I wonder if Christianity is a death cult. For a Chinese person, the image of the crucified Christ, there in churches across the land, is the most morbid and terrifying sight. How can I begin to understand the purpose of this imagery? There are some things about the West that just go over my head.

Gorbachev and the Curtain Rod

I feel like I have become one of the churchmen who copied the *Anglo-Saxon Chronicle*. I have noted down quite a number of political events in the last several months in my diary. Well, not a diary, it is a notebook I keep in my Hastings flat. I stopped my diary-writing habit after the birth of my child several years ago. For a while, as a new mother, I was unable to read or sleep properly, let alone think or write. Even though I had kept a diary since I was a teenager (and I believe that is part of the reason I evolved into the kind of writer I am today). I put my diary on the upper level of a bookshelf. Practicality has taken over my mental life. Only this year, I have managed to steal some time away from London and my child. I've begun to record things in my notebook. Nothing personal really. The date of the plumber over to replace the old boiler, or the increase in the council bill, or new energy bills, things like that. But one entry reads: 'Need to attend to that curtain rod. Gorbachev just died.'

Indeed, on 30 August 2022, Mikhail Gorbachev died in Moscow, at the age of ninety-one. His death triggers memories about my university days in China in the early 1990s. Gorbachev was discussed in our daily news and conversations during those years. In post-Mao China, people held him in great regard, though not his predecessors or successors. I thought of my father who was born in the same year as Gorbachev. He was one of the many Chinese

Communist Party members who admired Gorbachev and his reforms, even though the idea of a defunct Soviet Union was something incomprehensive for my father. But really, this part of Russian history remains incomprehensible for most Chinese people. Because we could only learn what had been released in the state media, and we have no true grasp of other countries' internal politics, especially a country like Russia.

The BBC airs a documentary about Gorbachev in his final years. It is a very sympathetic portrait. The old man sang Russian and Ukrainian songs in his living room. He also recited Russian poetry at the dinner table before boiled potatoes. Ah, potatoes, I could not help but pay attention to the dishes laid in front of him. Too many potato dishes! Not good for the heart or if you have diabetes. Maybe that is one of the reasons for Russian history suffering from a heavy heartbeat, metaphorically speaking. A genuine politician from old times, Gorbachev reminds me of our Chinese leader Deng Xiaoping, another politician who opened up an ideologically rigid country with his reforms after Mao. Both lived to a great age, almost a century long. Both reminded elderly people in their country of those 'good old days'. But I am too young to state such a thing. And I don't have the perspective of a citizen who has spent their life in one country.

3 September: the Tory Party members cast their final vote for a new leader. Even though everyone already suspects the dreary outcome.

5 September: Liz Truss is announced as the new prime minister. Her smile, according to some people in the streets, is 'charmless'. I did not realise that Liz Truss went to Oxford, just like many other high-profile English politicians. Is there only one place that produces British politicians? What happened to the diverse multicultural post-colonial society?

6 September: US Intelligence says Russia is buying millions of rockets and shells from North Korea, while Boris Johnson makes

his farewell speech in Downing Street with a slogan: 'We will come out stronger.'

What will happen tomorrow, and next week, and next month? The country which I have adopted as my home cannot be saved, nor is there a revolution on the horizon. No hope. Mouths talking, but their words mean nothing. It feels that most events in the Western democratic world are transitional and merely performative. Of course in the East, in countries like China, the politicians have performed their roles all along. But without the frequent election cycle, it allows the leaders to accomplish certain tasks, such as building national railways or improving health care. Though with Xi Jingping and Putin, my view has already been proved wrong. But still, I wonder how politicians can accomplish anything in this kind of political world. Perhaps Gorbachev would have something to say about it. Too bad. He's passed away.

4
Autumn

The Queen is Dead

8 September. In the morning hours, Buckingham Palace releases news that the Queen is 'under medical supervision'. Then the media reports that royal family members are on their way to their Scottish palace. I go out for a walk around the Old Town of Hastings.

A few hours later, not long after I return home, I turn on the radio. First I hear the national anthem playing, the tone mournful. What? I ask myself. So quick? It can't be! I turn up the volume. It is true, the news officially announces that the Queen is dead. I listen while eating a slice of mature Cheddar. The cheese is past its sell-by date and was reduced in Marks & Spencer. It is not dissimilar from the royal family, I think, though the difference is that one has persisted way, way beyond its expiry date, and is still very expensive. Motionless, I eat the Cheddar, looking at the cold rain and wind-blasted waves outside. Such is my protected modern existence, at this moment entirely reduced to the consumption of cow's milk. Really, we should worship cows and sheep, and not our kings and queens.

Then I hear Liz Truss making her official speech about the death of the Queen: 'She is the rock on which modern Britain was built . . .' I thought, rock? A rock of the country? One doesn't need to be a socialist to know that the real rock is the people. People only. The suffragettes, the trade unionists, the scientists, the street cleaners, the soldiers and sailors, the immigrants, the nurses, the teachers, the foreigners! Royalty is the icing on the cake.

I listen to more news. One disaster after another. Inflation. Flood. Energy crisis. Nuclear threat. Nevertheless, the new prime minister always smiles. She has this sharp look but with a touch of womanliness. Her clothing is neat in strong primary colours. She does not wear a flowery dress, at least never in public. Though of course all this is of little consequence seen against her economic policies. But she is a woman prime minister, a fact which is unavoidable, as she is subjected to the scrutiny of fashion critics. Everyone thinks she has modelled herself on Thatcher. The gossip rags have pulled out old photos of Thatcher to compare her style with Truss's. For example, both wore the same black blazer and white shirt with a large bow on the chest, both wore a royal-blue dress, and so on. Forty years on, the fashion industry doesn't seem to have been very inventive with female leaders' choice of clothes. But then the economic policies haven't changed much either. They can be summed up in one simple mantra, which Liz might mumble to herself when trying on her latest outfit: enrich the rich.

Strangely, an image of William the Conqueror trying on his chainmail comes to my mind now. Reaching for his sword he mutters: enrich the rich. The rich for the conqueror were his northern kinsmen, while Truss's rich are the hedge fund Tory donors.

Still, life goes on, even after the death of the Queen. And the flux of the seasons continues, despite the turbulence of British politics. As William Wordsworth said, nature does not betray you. One can only trust nature, nothing else. The autumn chill has not settled in yet, but the air smells different. As I take a walk through St Leonards Garden this morning, I notice that the red fuchsia is still blooming happily with their elongated petals. They show no sign of withering. I also see many birds – warblers and even some sparrows – chirping away on the meadow. I learn that the migratory birds may eventually stop flying south for the winter as they spend longer in their European breeding grounds. And according to birdwatchers, birds crossing the Sahara are now spending about sixty fewer days per year in Africa. The warming climate, perhaps, is so much more evident to the birds than to us humans. It's becoming more obvious to the birds that they don't need to move south. But if the migratory birds stop migrating, will their bodies grow larger and heavier and their wings become redundant one day? Possibly. I imagine chicken-like creatures with minute wings scurrying about swampy English forests.

Though some things don't change much. The seascape is unique here. The Hastings shoreline and its beaches are basically the same as they were a thousand years ago. So are the forests and hills along the Channel. Even the ruins of Hastings Castle, from the Roman times until today, which I climb from time to time, are still standing, despite almost collapsing completely at some point in history. But the ruins and rocks stay. The ruins are even expanding as those rocks and ferns become part of them, and they in turn become part of the new cityscape, part of my daily walks.

Bluetits

Without a curtain, I wake up with natural light. It is always earlier than I should like. Around seven this morning, I have already drunk enough coffee and finished a bowl of cereal. I am on my way to the beach.

The sun is struggling to get out from a belt of heavy clouds. I feel cold, but at least there is no wind. The tide is low and the soft sand bed stretches far and wide. It is peaceful. I walk on the watery surface of the shore. There are empty shells from razor clams, broken apart. There are small white clams too, and black mussels. But all their shells are empty, as if the night has stolen their bodies, leaving behind ghostly shells during the day. Perhaps they will recover their bodies again, this evening, this very night.

A number of people are settling down behind me. They put their stuff on the dry part of the beach, against the wooden-structured barriers. I have seen them before. They are a group of local swimmers, all women, all healthy-looking and tanned. Some are in their forties, but mostly they are middle-aged. Everyone carries a semi-professional swim kit. In no time, they have removed their fleece jackets and are half naked. They must have put on their swimming suits at home before adding the outer layers. Water boots, swimming gloves. I know the sea temperature is painfully cold during the autumn months, even though I barely dip my toes in. But they are Bluetits, the famous female cold-water swimming group. They are a wonder of the wintery beach.

This time they aren't carrying their flag. One evening, a few weeks ago, in a cold blasting storm, I saw these people moving about on the beach with a flag. It was the first time I became aware of such a group. Then I noticed that all of them were women, in their fifties, sixties and seventies. Some might have been even older. None of them looked unfit. The flag was flying beside a blue tent, which was put up by two women. On the flag there was a red-bellied finch, and the wording: Bluetits Chill Swimmers. And that was the first time I learned the word 'bluetits' was associated with them.

Since then I have seen the group often. One time, I saw two women swimming naked even though it was raining and the wind was howling. Though the water might have been warm that day. What these chill swimmers really need is not a bikini but a wetsuit, rubber gloves, socks and hat to cope with potential hypothermia.

Experienced swimmers may not die from drowning but might from hypothermia – as they can lose the ability to move after a while in the icy water.

And how do I learn to live in a cold climate? It is a question I often ask myself. The Chinese province where I grew up is semi-tropical with no winter. We did not call our jasmine 'winter jasmine' as the jasmine would flower all year round, so did our roses. I never needed to wear gloves or a padded jacket. But here, half of the year is winter. Perhaps to learn to live in a new climate is to embrace the environment even if it is harsh. In the end it is to do with adapting. One day I will be part of this brave and honourable scene. And I will become one of these women, a Bluetit. But right now, I am not. Maybe my negative state will last for a long time; it might last for the rest of my life. I do not know yet.

William's Army

Rubens' *Consequences of War* has been on my mind again. Such a strange and theatrical painting. It has all the symbols we associate with war, but none of the reality. It is grotesque, a kind of florid pornography, especially the naked bodies of the women contrasted with the men in armour. But though wars involve armies, Rubens wasn't interested in depicting them.

Since I was young, armies have just been images on television and cinema screens, they are barely real to me. So hard and machine-like, I was not attracted to the images at all. Even though we were drenched with slogans such as 'Fight for your country', I had no understanding about the nature of armies. But now I am researching the military facts around the Battle of Hastings, I am keen to know more about the two opposing armies that confronted each other in 1066. I read some historical accounts, but the knowledge refuses to stay in my mind, even though my eyes take in the words and numbers. I find the facts are dead and dry. I cannot feel much about a war so remote, so long ago. This is very different from the current war – Putin's war in Ukraine. It's ever-present, despite the fact that I am living on the corner of the European map. But there is not much distance between Russia and Britain when it comes to modern warfare.

I went to the local museum again, the place that taught me about the ancient Haestingas people. I hope to find more military information, at least visually.

This time, it has an art exhibition featuring local painters. I find myself in the midst of its opening reception. Everyone seems to know everyone else. As usual, I don't know anyone. I look at some landscape paintings, half-heartedly.

I am standing in front of a seascape painting with a shingle-dotted beach and pale pink waves when I hear a man's voice:

'Are you one of the painters too?'

I turn round, to see an elderly bearded man with a slim bottle of pale ale in his hand. I shake my head.

'You're not from here, are you?'

He seems to be at ease in this space, unlike me. I don't want to appear to be like a tourist, nor do I want to say I am a Londoner as some locals loathe Londoners, or FILTH – Failed in London, try Hastings. So I just smile vaguely.

'I am sort of local,' I explain humbly.

He laughs: 'A new local!'

He introduces himself as Ian. He is part of the show, not as a painter but as a frame-maker. He makes frames for some of the painters. As a fair exchange, I tell him I am a writer, who is here doing research about Anglo-Saxon history.

'Anglo-Saxon history.' Ian smiles, betraying surprise, white eyebrows arching. His beard is long and grey. He looks like a medieval monk, one who likes drinking ale – as did most of those monks who wrote the chronicle and other religious books.

'Which Anglo-Saxon history? As in Alfred the Great, King Cnut, or the Battle of Hastings?'

I nod at the last.

'Ha! You're in the right place, I would say. My younger brother is a historian, though I think I know most of the stuff he knows.'

For the next hour, I try to dig out what Ian knows about 1066. I would also like to learn more about his frame-making, but I don't have time to get into that topic. Ian seems to know quite a lot about William the Conqueror, though not much about King Harold, the last Anglo-Saxon king. It's true, I remind myself, that we only learn the winner's history and not the loser's.

'The Normans were originally Vikings! So they really knew how to build ships and how to kill. Those ships were called longboats, and were built from oak, ash or elm. Well, my brother the historian will tell me I am wrong about that. But I bet they had to use the same oak we use here!'

Ian's bottle is empty – time for another drink. I spot the last bottle of beer on the serving table. I go to grab it for him, since the reception looks like it's about to finish.

'I used to help the fishermen build their boats, so I know a bit about these kinds of things,' Ian remarks, drinking from his new bottle of ale. 'I bet the Normans knew how to secure their stern-posts with copper rivets and fasten their timber with iron nails . . .'

I don't want to interrupt, but he goes into a long speech about iron nails and copper rivets, which I have no interest in. He even tells me about the poor quality of rivets and nails that the Chinese manufacture and export to the West these days.

'They're really shit quality, you can screw up your work if the nails aren't straight,' he complains, his beard shaking from his speech.

I try to distract him from the topics of nails and rivets, hoping he will return to William's fleet and army.

When I walk home from the museum, I am carrying a piece of napkin, with a list Ian has made for me. His handwriting is clear and certain, just like the way he speaks.

William's army consisted of:
>   *Cavalry;*
>   *Infantry;*
>   *Archers;*
>   *Crossbowmen.*

Army clothing:
>   *The cavalrymen were clad in heavy chainmail hauberks, knee-length, with slits (to allow for riding);*
>   *The infantrymen wore chainmail;*
>   *The archers wore chainmail.*

Weapons:
>   *The infantry carried javelins or long spears;*
>   *Double-edged swords;*
>   *Shields made of metal and wood;*
>   *The archers had long bows or crossbows.*

People and objects on the ships:
>   *Knights and their servants;*
>   *Soldiers and their weapons and clothing;*
>   *Carpenters, smiths, cobblers, saddlers;*
>   *Rope-makers, tool-makers, arrowsmiths;*
>   *Cooks, fighting men, workmen, religious men;*
>   *Quantities of food and fresh water;*
>   *Spiced wine;*
>   *Tents;*
>   *Prostitutes.*

I am very impressed by the list Ian produced. He seems to know a lot about medieval warfare. I am surprised by his ending on prostitutes. That's very thorough thinking from a man's point of view. Perhaps he was also going to become a historian like his brother but for some reason he took up a manual job instead? The mere fact of listing carpenters, smiths, saddlers, etc., surely meant he had done some study of medieval history. Ironically, Ian didn't tell me anything about Harold and the English forces. So I have some list-making to do for myself.

Harold's Forces

In China, martial arts had always been a skill for men to learn. The Boxer Rebellion was one of the typical cases that men practised martial arts to fight. Even though China invented gunpowder as early as the ninth century, ordinary Chinese people could not possess guns and still cannot possess guns today. So the art of physical fighting has remained a good skill to learn in my country.

Men have always invented tools and weapons throughout history. But sometimes I wish that fighting could be transformed into a contest of martial arts. If one has to kill, better to kill artfully. And if living is not a poetic act, then at least death will be a poetic gesture.

The above thoughts are born during my research on King Harold Godwinson's military force, and how he tried to defeat the Norman invasion. I am getting there, though medieval military history is an awful landscape for me to appreciate. I really prefer a picture of men with swords or barehanded fighting in a minimal form in a bamboo forest, like the scenes you might see in a Chinese martial arts film. A wise man knows that to conquer he does not have to kill. He just has to show his superior knowledge of strategy and the enemy. As Sun Tzu announced 2,500 years ago, the master of war has true victory in avoiding battle altogether.

Instead of indulging in fantasies about the world of martial arts and the wisdom of Sun Tzu, I read about King Harold's army from a pile of old books. The exact number of soldiers in Harold's army is unknown. The contemporary records do not give reliable figures. The Normans exaggerate with 400,000 men on Harold's side; more modest estimates suggest 10,000 men. Those soldiers are more of history's nameless. Those who live and die without any archival record. Extraordinarily, there are only twenty named individuals that were assumed to have fought with Harold at Hastings. Just twenty men who deserve names. They include Harold's brothers, Gyrth and Leofwine, and two other relatives. Only the nobles get their names recorded.

The English army consisted entirely of infantry. I am going to make a list here, following Ian the frame-maker's method. I find listing is useful when trying to remember dry facts.

Harold's army:
> *Each soldier's equipment consisted of:*
> *a conical helmet;*
> *a metal ring hauberk;*
> *a shield;*
> *usually a two-handed axe;*
> *a sword.*

The English army was made up of professional soldiers and levies from the *fyrd*, a non-professional people lightly armoured. To me, they would have been better off if they had known martial arts and trained their horses. Poor King Harold, if only he had gone to a Taoist country in the East to learn the art of fighting, he might have saved old Anglo-Saxon England.

Most of Harold's infantry would have formed part of the shield wall, in which all the men in the front ranks locked their shields together. Behind them would have been axemen and soldiers with javelins as well as archers. But if the wall broke, everything fell apart quickly. And that's exactly what happened, apparently.

Humans are imaginative animals. I wonder whether some foot

soldiers, in their dying moments on miserable battle fields, hallucinate about super-weapons that could destroy everything, themselves as well as their enemies. Putting an end, immediately, to all suffering and all victory. Annihilation. Or, do they pray to their gods, whoever they are? Or, do they think of their warm cottages and wives, their dogs and fireplaces, their children and their fields? Or maybe simple meaningless patterns appear triggered by the mud, blood and shredded flesh their eyes dully see, as their minds slowly move towards extinction?

Sharks and Whales

For the last few days, Moon and her father have joined me for the school break. We spend most of our time outside, walking endlessly from the beaches to the hills. The child complains about her sore feet, but is happy to pick up kilos of seashells and rocks to stuff into her school bag. This morning, before they take the train back to London, Moon sees a baby shark on the rugged beach. She calls to us, in horror and excitement.

It is grey in colour, its little body pale, with a spotty patterned long tail. Fresh blood oozes from its jaw all the way to the belly. I can see no cut – perhaps it has bled from the gills? Every part of its body is intact. The fins are perfect. Looking at the shape of the tail, I imagine how it would have thrust and swung when it was alive.

'Was it killed by a dog?' Moon asks. 'Do dogs like to eat fish?'

We have neither dogs nor cats at home.

'Or it was killed in the sea?'

'The blood wouldn't be so fresh if it had already been killed in the sea. Maybe it was killed by humans during the low tide,' I answer.

On the way to the train station, the child talks about sharks and whales with her father, while I clutch her heavy school bag under my arm. Stones, shells and Harry Potter books are the treasures she will bring back.

'Sharks are fish, not mammals,' her dad explains. 'But they give birth through placentas.'

'So strange.' Moon frowns. 'You mean a baby shark grows inside its mother's body, getting juice and oxygen through a tube?'

'Yes, though an umbilical cord. The same as us mammals.'

Now the child becomes silent, probably picturing herself in a womb, connected to a cord. Or, she might be imagining an unborn sucking nutrients from its tiny surroundings, eyes closed, body twisted.

'But when the pups are born they're immediately independent and have to fend for themselves. They have to swim in the ocean to avoid being eaten at any second. Otherwise they would die.' Her father continues the social Darwinist education.

'Was that why this baby shark was attacked by a fisherman or a monster fish?'

The train has arrived. It left Ore ten minutes late. Passengers now move towards the edge of the platform impatiently. Most of them are Londoners, I can tell from their dress and their chatter. The child and her father jump onto it.

'Come back on Wednesday, or I will miss you, Mum,' the child says.

I nod vaguely. It depends on how much progress I have made with my writing. Alone, empty-handed, I start walking home. I take a detour, passing by the beach.

The shark reminded me of something else.

A local swimmer told me that she once saw a dead white whale, washed up on the beach, during one of her morning plunges. How did it die? I asked her. They have lost their sonic senses, she answered, because the sea is too noisy for them! The sea is too noisy? I was intrigued by her insider's knowledge, and went home to read about the noise in the sea to understand what she meant. Apparently, whales use their sonic abilities to detect the activities around them. For most whales and for many fish, eyes are only occasionally useful. Whales make whistles and squeaks, they echo-locate to communicate information with each other and detect the movement of fish around them. But now there are so many container ships and oil-drilling machines in the ocean, the sensitivity of the sea creatures' sensors has been dulled. If a whale is within two hundred metres of a container ship or a hundred metres of a boat with an outboard engine, its sensors can be completely lost. Some industry vessels produce noise all night and all day, and are often most active and loudest at night. So the ocean is very noisy, and the noise is amplified below the surface. Poor whales and sharks, turning round and round in the disturbed water, losing their survival skills after millions of years of evolution.

Monks and Writers

The days grow shorter. A sense of anxiety grows in me. I must spend less time walking endlessly on the hills and beaches, but more time on writing and reading. Otherwise I will never get to that October day in 1066, to the Battle of Hastings. Though I am making progress, I am slightly stuck in the September of 1066.

That September, Harold Godwinson defeated his brother Tostig in the north. Now William was Harold's only serious opponent. Reading through the chronicle, I cannot find many authentic personal details about William, or much about King Harold. The churchmen who wrote the chronicle in their cave-like dwelling do not seem to have been in awe of these 'great' figures. Their way of thinking was stoic and perhaps historical coherence was never their intention. Whereas I am a naive sentimentalist, and I always want to connect the events with some sense of narrative. I even invest my emotions in a history that has nothing to do with *my* history. I need to believe that there is something for me to find there, something wonderful that is yet to come. If I know how to look, how to read properly, or how to think faster, and if I live in Hastings long enough, I will internalise this history, physically and intellectually. Embodiment, assimilation, integration – these are big words, but they seem to name a stage or a state I ought to be able to achieve in my brief life. Some day in the future, perhaps.

The churchmen would have laboured away beside a burning

candle, their bread stale and cold. I sit by my double-glazed aluminium window, reading and making notes. I am a writer who has spent most of my adult life writing, not unlike those monks in the church. Though I write in an adopted language. My writing always begins with the process of translating, or self-translating.

It has been cold for several weeks now. In what season did the monk note down the events of the year 1066? How much time passed before some other chronicler came on the scene and revised the details, toiling beside another lit candle, another stale loaf of bread? What seems to be consistent is the way in which they paid great attention to numbers. The numbers killed. The number of horsemen. The number of boats. The number of days, or, more often, the number of winters. I love the numbering of winters in the chronicle. When it comes to the killing, the writer shows no hint of feeling, merely recording the facts of the slaughter. '*The enemy then made a great slaughter there – about four hundred or five hundred men; they on the other side none.*' The repeated use of the word 'slaughter' and the words 'slew' and 'slain' creates a kind of brutal, street-style poetry. I am very aware that what I am reading is a modern translation of Old English. I do not know the original word for either 'slay' or 'slaughter' in Old English, I need yet to learn. But even to my ears, attuned (though ever more distantly) to different sounds of different monks, these words – slew and slain – seem archaic, terrible but beautiful, and lodge somewhere inside me.

Pevensey

The morning feels frigid, with the temperature down to 7 or 8 degrees. The day unfolds with sunny intervals, as the sky becomes brighter. The sea is the same blue-grey, but the news is bad. Ordinary Russians are fleeing to Georgia in order to escape the national mobilisation. Gas is leaking into the Baltic Sea and the Swedish are investigating the sabotage of the Nord Stream pipeline. The pound is hitting an all-time low. I turn off the radio. As I leaf through my notes, I notice I wrote 'Pevensey' in huge letters. Almost one thousand years ago, William the Conqueror crossed the Channel and landed at Pevensey. That's right! The Normans arrived in Pevensey first, not in Hastings. Only twelve miles away, Pevensey is very close to where I am now, but I have never visited the place.

Next day, as I am meeting my child and her father at the station, I make a quick decision.

'Where are we going?' Moon asks, already looking impatient. She has changed from her school uniform into a dress, ready for a beach weekend.

'To a town called Pevensey. It's very close, I promise.'

Her father frowns, taking out his phone. He begins checking Google Maps.

'Is that right, only ten minutes away?' He raises his head from the phone.

'Actually, nine minutes.'

The child is still resisting the idea of another journey.

'I promise I'll buy a big ice cream for you once we get there.' I take her school bag and lead her back onto the platform. 'Any flavour you like.'

'Can I have a chocolate one, with sprinkles on it?'

'Of course.'

Fifteen minutes later, we are in Pevensey. Moon has a chocolate ice cream with sprinkles as promised, Steve has a takeaway – fish and chips. We walk on the narrow pavement, in a disorderly way. To anyone local, we must look totally non-local.

Nevertheless, I try to pay attention to the surroundings. The small village centre of Pevensey is charmingly laid out. So small, the 'high street' does not look like a high street. Most of the premises are small, low in height. The doors of the cottages are even smaller, miniature.

'They look like the home of Snow White and the seven dwarfs,' Moon remarks.

'Or like the homes of Hobbits,' her father counters.

I wonder how different the dwellings were during the tenth or eleventh century – presumably not much bigger. I imagine Vikings trying to smash through tiny doors, too small for their own bulk. Though the chimney structures are rather big compared with the other parts of the houses. I imagine the fireplaces in each house, and Santa Claus hanging on the chimney top looking down every Christmas. This place might be a wonderfully mythical place to grow up in. How would a Chinese know?

In fact, it's like a living theme park. I notice that most of the cottages are named. As I pass the rose-hedged front gardens, I read their signs: Banks Lodge, Searoad Cottage, Primrose House, April Cottage. Then we pass a solemn Tudor-looking white house calling itself Post Office Cottage. It has a green post box by its door, quaint archways and an inner maze-like courtyard. I feel like I am returning to medieval England. What's that phrase? It's living anachronism.

I need to get more familiar with this idea of past and present super-imposed on each other. The past has not been scorched from the earth, like in China.

It's not long before we reach the castle, which looms before us: open ruins exposed on a hill. There is a circular architecture with broken walls and a watchtower. We read the tourist information board and learn it was built by the Romans. Perhaps that's why William the Conqueror made sure to take over the place right after the conquest. The grass is tall and lush around the castle ruins. Away from the traffic, the fields feel peaceful, preserved from the ravages of time. There is a certain atmosphere, which leaves me groping for words to describe it. Moon throws herself on the soft grass, rolling and messing about. Her father wanders off with a look of distraction. He may be time-travelling too.

This place was meant to be where the Norman armies landed. But we are now some distance from the sea, which can barely be glimpsed. A thousand years ago, Pevensey was a peninsula, but it is now a mile inland from the bay. It takes thirty minutes to walk from the castle to the sea, if one knows the quick route. On the one hand, things have changed, people and nature. But on the other, the broad contours of the landscape remain much the same. A thirty-minute walk down to the sea is nothing compared to a history containing a thousand-year-old event. For me, this thirty-minute walk is like going back in time. It is magical but also perplexing.

In order to land in this area in 1066, the Duke of Normandy had prepared a vast fleet. I read that it took nine months and a large number of labourers to build such a fleet. Nine months, that's the same length of time as a woman's pregnancy. Though the latter produces a child, the birth of new life, the former produced only bloodshed, murder and sorrow, and the mad satiation of greed.

Two hours later, we hesitate on a winding street outside the ruined castle. We ponder if we should take a coffee break here, or return to Hastings straight away. The child wins the battle. She says she absolutely wants to go back to Hastings, so she can play on the beach and look for her lost doll. As for the doll, its fate is probably already sealed. She forgot it somewhere on the beach near St Leonards almost a month ago. We head back, via a different route, but get lost on the plain below the castle hill, which had once been the sea.

Armageddon

On my morning walk, I found a plastic doll on the beach. It was not the doll my child had lost a month ago. It was a Barbie, brown curly hair, half naked, skinny with all the typical characteristics. Well, children always lose their dolls, I thought to myself. I walked around it, without picking it up. Then I walked further, passing two or three swimmers. They were just coming back from their swim, and had wrapped themselves well, in hooded bathing robes.

It is getting chilly. The maples and oaks in St Leonards Garden are turning yellow. The ducks in the pond are disappearing. Night winds come, sweeping the wilted leaves across the wet soil. Walking in the rainy autumnal streets makes me feel despondent. But I have no choice. One cannot change the weather, just as Cnut could not command waves despite his regal power. I read and write for an hour at home, but it feels cold without turning on the heating. I put on another sweater and think of a warm place to go where I can continue my labours. I remind myself that a new cafe has opened on King's Road. It plays the kind of jazz and blues I like. Bringing the chronicle and my diary, I close the door behind me.

As I descend the spiral staircase I hear a dog barking behind a closed door. I have not seen my downstairs neighbour, the red-haired old lady with her dog, for a while. I cannot help but wonder if she is all right.

I walk through the drizzle wearing my long raincoat. No

umbrella. Anyone who holds an umbrella along this coast must be from some inland place with still air. All umbrellas here are turned inside out by the savage gusts. I enter the cafe. Someone is sitting by the window, having a Korean-style lunch. A fried egg laid on a mix of rice, kimchi and beef, everything in little portions but inviting. Well, I shall order the same thing. While waiting for my food, I pick up a local newspaper. The front page announces that the number of people who have made the dangerous journey across the Channel in small boats this year is double the total for all of last year. Then there is mention of the figure: *At least 819 migrants succeeded in reaching the UK on Sunday.*

Most of these migrants probably landed on the shingle beach of the Kent coast, somewhere desolate and less populated like Dungeness beach. But there must have been some who were blown in my direction, along Felixstowe and Hastings. For these people on small boats, such as dinghies and even kayaks – I could hardly believe it when I saw a picture of refugees in one kayak – the English Channel is a fatal combination of danger and hope. I imagine overloaded boats, dark turbulent water, heads and arms streaked by freezing spray, children huddled and crying . . . Survival or death.

There is a *Guardian* on the table too. I take a quick look at the front page. Two headlines catch my eye. First, President Joe Biden says the world could face Armageddon if Putin uses nuclear weapons to win the war in Ukraine. The second is that the number of butterflies in the UK fell to the lowest level in the last thirteen years. Here we go, Armageddon and no butterflies! What should we do and how should we live, in order to *continue* to live in this world? We can send a man (or woman) to the moon but we cannot deal with an ageing Russian man's inferiority complex. Maybe finding a way to save butterflies would help us to find a way to prevent imminent Armageddon? The incredible 'butterfly effect' in chaos theory is something that springs to mind. How are the butterflies doing in Russia, I wonder, among bushes and trees in the Ural

Mountains? Perhaps no one in Russia now has the time or luxury to count the numbers of butterflies in their region. And would there be anybody left in the country if the war continued for another year? Would another Tolstoy be born in order to write the *War and Peace* of our times? Very likely, and probably already. Someone stoic (hiding in Siberia or on Sakhalin Island) is writing a masterwork at this very moment, while the atrocities are being carried out in Ukraine. Tolstoy was a butterfly-loving man, after all.

I think of those monks in medieval times who tried to record historical events, the overthrowing of kings or the merging of nations. Some were consumed by Tolstoyan passion and devotion. Others might have been detached in their approach. Like modern civil servants composing propaganda for their employers, simply earning a wage. My Korean lunch arrives. I find a pair of chopsticks and some soy sauce. I reflect that it's all the same. The world is getting closer to Armageddon but we are indifferent, and life goes on, at least lunch goes on. Who knows what will happen after lunch? I stab the rice with my chopsticks. While I munch on the kimchi, I check the time, in case Armageddon really is imminent. It is two in the afternoon. After lunch, I say to myself, I should go and have a look at the sea. I would like to check where the tide is. If it is high tide, we will be swept away effortlessly in the very moment of Armageddon. It would be painless, at least compared to other forms of death.

Re-enactment

15 October. It is a significant weekend – a re-enactment of the 1066 battle is to be held in Battle Abbey. I now know that this re-enactment in October is an annual affair in memory of the Norman Conquest a thousand years ago. What a strange and wonderful idea. I wonder if something like this could only be invented in Britain, a country that sees the great defeat of their past as a comedy show, as entertainment, a weekend outing for the families. I am (almost) sure that the Chinese or the French don't have such a cool attitude towards a past defeat. It requires a huge detachment from history, from a collective past, to be able to make tragedy into comic entertainment. I must admit that this is one of the good qualities the British have.

For such an important historical education, I have booked a

family ticket for the three of us, a small foreign tribe hidden among locals.

Arriving in the town of Battle early in the morning, we hope to avoid the queues. Once inside, we are amazed by the size and grandeur of the abbey, its fields, its monastery, its orchard, its walled rose garden, as well as the dense wood sloping down the surrounding hills. But first of all, the child needs to have some sugar in her stomach before agreeing to ingest a whole day's worth of history (somehow she doesn't believe it will be entertaining for her). So we look for a tea shop with cakes. In the museum cafe, we discover that even the food menu is full of historical-inspired specialities, Saxon Oat Cake and Norman Spiced Cake and the like. I order a Saxon Oat Cake to share with Steve. Moon has a whole sandwich for herself as well as a slice of Norman Cake.

The show lasts all day but the throngs are already arriving in the early-morning hours. There are so many French-speaking tourists, which surprises us. I didn't think that the French would care to see their ancestors' victory on English soil in such a 'real' form. Well, perhaps all this is due to the positive reputation (or the effective advertising) of the re-enactment. It is well curated for someone who is witnessing the event for the first time. Various activities and performances are scheduled for the morning hours. There is a falconry show named 'The Noble Art of Hawking', and an 'Iron and Fire' performance to show how knives were made during medieval times (and why so many people are named Smith). There is a 'Cavalry and Infantry Display' with costumed actors in a spectacular open field. They are incredibly vivid when they put on chainmail, helmets and masks. But all this is happening under drizzling rain, and none of us have brought an umbrella or raincoat. We wander from one show to another, half impressed and half frozen, on the once blood-drenched muddy fields of English history.

The afternoon arrives. We are wet and cold. But the final re-enactment is yet to come. To console the child, we agree to buy some marshmallows for her to take to an open fire pit. I have never seen such a large marshmallow, stuck on a long barbecue stick. Here she is, happily roasting her treat by an open fire with the other kids. The rain is no longer bothering her.

By the time re-enactment begins, everyone is weary, consumed by such a long wait. As I chat with the people around us, they seem to have come from everywhere: Ireland, Scotland, Scandinavia, India, China, America. Most of them carry high-tech camera equipment, some even with a makeshift chair. Though not us, the little tribe. Damp and frozen, we three squat on the grass and watch the show. The battle is conducted just as I have imagined it so many times. Still, it is impressive to see well-trained actors on horseback (the Normans) and as foot soldiers (the Anglo-Saxons) standing close together, forming a shield wall. The performance is finished within twenty-five minutes, but the incredible amount of actors, costumes, music, as well as horses they have used is something that deserves a big applause. Though one thousand years ago, even from the Norman side, it would hardly have been a collective joy given the sheer horrors of tens of thousands of corpses lying around mixed with dead animals on a dark autumn day. In a way, what happens in front of us has nothing to do with history, but to do with a meticulous sense of theatrical production. Shakespeare would have approved. It is a land of Shakespearean existence. Even the Saxon Oat Cake, perhaps even the giant marshmallow, even the dripping wet grass on the slopes of hills dotted by sheep dung – all this is a re-enactment of an ongoing past. Theatre is what the British are good at. History is spectacle.

TOAST YOUR OWN
MARSHMALLOWS

October, the Tory Turmoil

20 October. Tory MPs call upon the new prime minister to step down. This seems to be beyond my comprehension. In the West, they can change their prime minister every month. No wonder no politician can carry out any policy, let alone make long-term plans. All he or she should worry about is if their job will be taken away the next day. There is more pressing news, on Russia and Ukraine, but I need some food. I fry some salmon (imported from Iceland). I have just finished eating the gingered salmon when I check the news again. BREAKING NEWS: Liz Truss has stepped down! Even more shocking, perhaps: the government announces that a new prime minister will be elected by next Friday!

What an October. Only a few days ago I witnessed the re-enactment of the Battle of Hastings, and this week the real theatre of British politics! It feels like the tenure of a British prime minister is shorter than my cooking and eating a salmon dish. Liz Truss was only forty-five days in office, the lifespan of a fruit fly. And now everybody in Parliament is hurrying to put on their best suits in order to race for the position of a new leader. Why not? Politics in the UK is a truly perfect theatre show. No wonder Britain produced the best playwright in the world. Shakespeare could not be Chinese or Korean.

Monday, 24 October, not even four days after Truss resigned, Britain already has its new prime minister! Rishi Sunak is back, all smiles, with a raised hand to thank the public. The stock market is calm, and has not crashed yet. A new prime minister within four days! No country can do something like this, really. In the evening, I turn on the radio for more news. Right after the announcement that Sunak will meet King Charles tomorrow, the BBC warns that there will be a partial solar eclipse in Europe in the morning. It will appear at 10.30 UK time and no one should look directly at the sun.

What strange double news! Sunak becomes the new prime minister at the very moment of a solar eclipse in Europe. Auspicious or ominous? When Harold Godwinson became the king of old Wessex, the comet shone in the sky for the whole week! But it only led Harold to dying within nine months. A short-lived king. Surely Sunak will last much longer. He is young, with great private health care.

I have witnessed the political turmoil in Britain. This is the year of the Battle of Hastings in modern times. The rapid change of prime ministers and the death of the Queen remind me of the Year of the Four Emperors. It was during the first civil war of the Roman Empire, when four emperors ruled in succession: Galba, Otho, Vitellius and Vespasian. All short-lived (except for Vespasian), and ill served. It is considered an important interval, marking the transition from the Julio-Claudian dynasty to the Flavian dynasty. The latter was known for its vast Roman temple-construction programme. I wonder what kind of future this Tory leadership change will bring. And if this is just a transitional period in British history, what would be the new era facing everyone?

My notebook is full, I will have to buy a new one soon. What I have now in my daily life is the ever-maddening news. The world is spinning but in a direction chroniclers (the news reporters) are uncertain of. All they can do is to note down the events and report as much as they can. But the difference between the old churchmen and the modern reporters is that the former recorded history with indifference under their master's interest, whereas the latter report the chaos with eagerness, participation and a sense of confusion. There is no distance between the reporting and the happening. All is happening in real time in front of our eyes, except that we must close our eyes as the solar eclipse is too strong.

No more sun. Since yesterday it has been raining. Now as I zigzag through alleyways in the drizzle, I notice shop windows decorated with pumpkins and Halloween items. I like seeing all sorts of pumpkins, small and large, green or golden, round and misshapen. But not so much the skeletons. The charity shops have put up some grotesque examples by the door. You can buy a skeleton for one pound fifty if you fancy having one in your house.

5
Winter

Bluetits Again

This is my second winter in Hastings. Now I count as an old Anglo-Saxon.

I have decided this winter that every day I will put my feet in the sea. It is not a problem on warm days. It is a real challenge in the freezing weather.

This evening when the cold mist starts to wrap around the beach, the women's swimming group arrives with their gear. As usual, they chat while taking off their clothes. There is always some distance between me and them, so that no one feels their territory is being intruded upon, even in this open space. Their territory seems to never change much. They prefer to stay beside a wooden barrier, where the line of breakwater extends all the way from the bank to the open sea. If you duck down behind the barrier, you feel less exposed to the harsh blow of gales. Though it is strange, I have never seen so many breakwater structures along European seashores, or Chinese seashores. The English coast seems to be full of these wooden groynes, as the locals call the breakwaters. I wonder how much erosion the English beaches would suffer without these fences.

I manage to take off my tights and walk in the icy water for a little bit. Perhaps two minutes this time. But pain starts to enter my bones. I have to get out. I return to the shingle area, and move towards the women swimmers. I am not sure why. Perhaps I want to chat with them, to feel part of the scene.

'How long do you normally stay in the water?' I ask one of the women, who is putting on her water gloves.

'Not very long. It depends. In this weather, some minutes if I have my swimming socks on,' she says.

I express my admiration.

Looking at my street clothes, she says: 'Are you going to join us?'

I nod, with a smile.

'Maybe I need a wetsuit,' I add, with some embarrassment.

'It might help. But you need to practise every day. Start with one minute. Gradually increase it. You'll get used to it eventually.'

Off she goes, passing along the ragged shingle and entering the white wavy water.

I stand in the salty wind, motionless, thinking. When I was younger, I thought a woman's life ended at the age of fifty. As I am approaching this age, I feel that I possess none of the qualities these women swimmers show me every time I see them on my beach. They are strong, fearless, embracing the weather and the environment, their beauty is not marked by superficiality but a deep dignity. They are part of history: this history, this landscape. They are the true mermaids of this seascape. Yet I stand here on this beach, fully clothed in my urban style, in my warm boots, vain and weightless. I have summoned myself, mustered myself, to come to live in this place, in this landscape. I must embrace it, I must take in everything I witness in front of me, in this freezing wind, on this rugged shore.

The Battle of Hastings

Why am I still trying to put together a picture around the Battle of Hastings? Have my efforts to research the topic also uncovered, accidentally, what it was that prompted me on this path? I feel like a child trying to understand how life and death manifest themselves, and if I understand that, then I will understand the history of a country, a kingdom, a people or a decisive battle which shaped the Britain of the last one thousand years.

Between men and men, they agreed to fight. All dressed up, mounted and weaponised. All fed, drank, vowed and ritualised. They agreed on a certain hour of a certain day. The battle on that October morning began at nine. This hour seems to be agreed by every historian. It must have been conveniently made up for entering into a historical record. To claim an exact hour to start a battle seems to me an absurd thing. The moment could be triggered by a sudden gust of howling wind, or a large eagle passing the duke's shoulder, or a cold raindrop on King Harold's eyebrow. All this could be a catalyst to launch an instant attack.

The Normans formed their army in three groups. The front lines were made up of archers, with foot soldiers armed with spears behind. The English formed a shield wall, with the foot soldiers holding their shields. Maybe William the Conqueror opened the battle with archers in the front, weakening the enemy with arrows. Then the infantry would engage in close combat. But most crucially, the

Normans had thousands of horses whereas the Anglo-Saxons didn't. The Norman cavalry would create openings in the English lines. Besides, the Normans also tricked the Anglo-Saxons by pretending to retreat, which caused a natural line break of English soldiers. Then William's cavalry could break through the English forces, killing and pursuing the fleeing soldiers. The poor local soldiers ended up scattering and dying on their own land.

I had looked in some record, and it said the sunset hour of that day was at 4.54 p.m. The English fields in the autumn would be almost dark by then. Did the killings slowly die down as the sky darkened? Was it rainy? Was it windy? How did the surviving soldiers feel trapped among the corpses when the night ascended? There would be no light illuminating the mountains and hills, even if the moon was shining, the battlefield would be pitch-black, loomed by tens and thousands of corpses. I imagine life on those hills. Rain in the forests and on the marshes. Insects on apple trees and diseased pear branches.

There are a few versions of how poor Harold was killed. First version was that Harold was killed by William the Duke himself – both revealed their faces under the helmets during the battle. This is certainly too convenient, almost cartoonish. The second was that Harold died by an arrow wound to the head. Another version was that Harold was targeted by four men – first he was pierced on his chest and then a second man chopped his head off while the other two cut off his thigh and dismembered him. And the most popular version, which was drawn in the Bayeux Tapestry, was that Harold was shot by an arrow to the eye and then he was cut down by a cavalryman. But in all these versions, no woman was present during the death of the last Anglo-Saxon king. Women characters were added later, for sentimental value, by artists and storytellers.

Since I am not a historian, I find I can't worry too much about the details of how Harold died. What I understand is a simple yet complex fact: the Normans had taken over England and a French era began in this part of the world.

After the 1066 conquest, it took at least thirty years for the French Normans to seize most English lands, killing vast numbers of locals to solidify their conquest. Legends claim that even the ruthless conqueror himself on his deathbed confessed that he annihilated the English and felt guilt-ridden. But this has been challenged by the historians who believe it is just the propaganda from William's confessor. You can read in different languages his final speech on his deathbed – in French, Latin, Norse, Old English and Modern English.

But what I understand is this: the conqueror led the obliteration of the old Anglo-Saxons and their cultures, and is one of the most chilling atrocities in history.

Father Tongue

Most Anglo-Saxon men were massacred during and after the Norman invasion. What about women though?

William's forces raped as many women as they could find after the battle. Raped and burned, that was the fate of most of local women – a standard practice in medieval times. But still, the Normans had to keep some young Anglo-Saxon women to serve them. For the next decades, the conqueror effectively replaced the local landowners with French aristocrats. Now a small number of foreign men ruled over the majority of the land and its people. There were hardly any Norman women following the Duke of William on his military campaign, nor would they cross the Channel dragging or abandoning their French-speaking children along with their wet nurses. So the French men in England, from knights to soldiers, had to 'use' the local English women. 'Use' is the word I think of for such a savage time, if I don't want to repeat the word 'rape' in every line. The rapes produced plenty of children. But these local women spoke English. The children were brought up by these women, speaking English at home, though their father tongue would be French. Perhaps those children wouldn't see themselves as the products of rape and war, as they would now be perceived in our modern society. After all, this was a thousand years ago. But still, there must have been an interesting dynamic between their father tongue and mother tongue, whether or not those children spoke both languages. And in most cases the children might have never learned who their real father was, but Norman French was the language they must have aspired to learn unless they were resigned to the fate of remaining peasantry like their defeated ancestors.

After the Norman invasion, the natives in England called themselves *les Engleis*, just as the Normans used to call the English. But after the conquest, more or less everyone was *les Engleis*. The French chevaliers married some of the remaining aristocratic native women, so they called themselves *les Engleis*. And their children from the intermarriage (who were the top crust of society) were the perfect *Engleis*, who would speak French and English. So in a wealthy household in Sussex, or in Kent, after lunch, when the father had gone out hunting and the mother was dealing with the servants, the son might say to his younger sister: 'Can you dire moi pourquoi tu aimes your silly poupées, passez-moi les boules, will you?' And if the sister was a fierce girl with some Viking blood, she might shout back: 'Eloigne-toi de moi, you merde!'

Is it too quick to make the conclusion that history is indeed a bastard, like the language we speak now, our supposed 'first' language and 'second' language? The 'first' and the 'second' could be just the other way around. We are the bastard of language – the languages of conqueror and conquered. I spoke Chinese in the past and now I speak English. Does that mean English has conquered my Chineseness? But even though I am now writing in English, I think in Chinese, or at least I *think* that I think in Chinese. I am never sure which language is controlling the other. I am a hybrid. And I am surprised that I don't feel any resentment or fear of losing my old language. I take the hybrid language as it is, very much like those children – *les Engleis* – who grew up in England after the Battle of Hastings. Bastard or hybrid, they were born, they grew and aged, then they died, but that is not the end – a new generation is born, with a different kind of hybridity.

Burials

I am still thinking about those dead bodies, multitudes of them, scattered around the fields of East Sussex after the battle. I wonder if those Anglo-Saxon soldiers – whether professional warriors or ordinary farmers – thought about how they would like to be buried. Perhaps some wanted to be buried on their farmland, along with their ancestors. Others might have hoped to be buried in a neighbouring village, in some spot that was special to them, along with their favourite dog or horse. Or to be buried under an old oak tree, or beside a sacred lake. I cannot know. All I know is that most of these soldiers died without a burial.

I think of a woman warrior from 3,200 years ago. Archaeologists discovered an ancient tomb in China that contained a large number of weapons. After painstaking research, they uncovered the identity of the buried person. Her name was Fu Hao. She was one of the wives of a king of the Shang Dynasty. As well as a fearless warrior, she was also a priestess who owned her own land. Her life is recorded on the oracle bones the archaeologists came across too. It reveals that she led many military campaigns to help the king against invading neighbours. The oracle bone inscriptions also show that the king repeatedly instructed Fu Hao to conduct special rituals and to offer sacrifices to the ancestors. In her tomb, there were nearly five hundred bronze objects, mostly weapons such as axes, knives, tiger heads, and 564 bone objects, including spears and arrowheads.

If I was a woman from old times, what would I be buried with? I ask myself. Perhaps I would feel safe if I lay beside a sharp knife, or a bow. But I might want to be buried among flowers and the most exquisite plants. But if I was a real Buddhist or a Taoist, I would not want to be buried with anything, or to be buried at all. I would not even think in those terms, knowing that all living things wither and darken under the earth, even though my ancient self might have believed in reincarnation.

For me, to be buried with objects is a denial of death. It is the hope to be reborn, or at least to have an afterlife. But I would not hope to continue a human-like life after my death. Not even an animal's life. All living beings with a mind cannot avoid going through suffering. I would rather be a tree, a river or a pebble. Or better, a nameless object in nature.

Warhorses

Occasionally, as I walk along the shore, I think of the warhorses on the stormy sea during the voyage in 1066. Did some horses get sick? And how did the horses react when they first landed on the sludgy English mud? Were they allowed a moment to graze the green grass of England? Or were they forced to charge and fight immediately after landing?

Most of the horses I have seen have been on country farms. They idle away, just like sheep or cows. They do little. On some farms in Essex and Sussex, they are used for riding lessons. But these are not warhorses. Of course, today there are barely any specially trained warhorses, a phenomenon that ended when modern artillery took over warfare.

Horses are very sensitive. When a man rides on its back, the animal can feel the pace of the master's heartbeat. The relationship, especially the trust between the rider and the animal, would have determined how they moved together and fought in battle. In the old days, a fighter relied on his horse as much as he relied on his sword. A fighter without a trained horse or a good sword was doomed to fail. This seems to be especially true in the case of the Battle of Hastings.

Warhorses would have been trained to such an extent that they became accustomed to weapons waving around their bodies. During a training session, the trainer would sit in the saddle of his horse, carrying a six-foot-long stick, its size and weight resembling a sword. As his legs sent messages to the horse for directing its movement, he would tap the horse's head, back and sides with his stick. He would pass the stick gently in front of his horse, especially in front of its eyes, from right to left, then left to right. In this way the horse would get used to the intrusion of a weapon. The key was to get the horse to face the enemy directly, so the man on the horse could see what was in front of him even when the animal was walking backwards or sideways to avoid the attack.

In ancient times, warhorses were smaller in size. Larger, heavier horses were more costly to maintain. But later, especially in Northern Europe, the horses needed to carry more armour, so men had to breed heavier, bigger horses. But just imagine: a man in hefty chainmail with a metal helmet and a sword as well as a metal shield is already very heavy for a horse to carry, let alone fight and run and manoeuvre around a dangerous battleground.

Since there is no more demand for warhorses, the animals have changed their profession. They are trained for racing. Once, on a visit to Salisbury, I met a jockey. He was lean and physically fit, a perfect build for a jockey. He told me that he had just retired, well, quit, really. Why did you quit? I asked. 'Well, I've been living with horses all my life, but I never owned my own horses. I trained and rode horses for rich people, so they could win races. But after twenty-odd years, I saw those horses die. You know, a horse can only live for so long. Each time I sensed an old horse was declining, coming close to death, I felt heartbroken.'

At that moment the jockey stopped speaking. We fell silent. I waited for the moment to pass. After some seconds, he carried on. Since then, he had wanted to raise his own horses, to live with them on his farm, not to train them for racing. 'You know, very often, after lunch, I lie on the ground at my farm, and my horses come, they stand quietly beside me, for a long time, as though we're doing double meditation,' he said. 'If I don't get up, my horses won't move.' He spoke those words slowly, beautifully. I will always remember that conversation.

Ukraine Flag

The sea is totally brown today. Muddy brown – a troubled look. Even though the sky is more or less blue, with clouds entangled in some parts. Where does this brownness come from? Has Southern Water released another deluge of human waste product? Or is it the chaotic confluence of tide, swell and wind? It seems that mud and sand have been carried by the wind from the sea onto the shore. Is the mud from Lower Normandy, another invasion?

The water is unmistakably freezing. I have just managed to take off my socks and dip my feet in. A sort of torture, a shock for the skin and bones. But the cold does good things for our bodies, otherwise why would the Bluetits and even the non-Bluetits come to this godforsaken place in the coldest season?

Clenching my teeth, I rush back to the shingle. Wind is whipping the coast violently. A ceaseless struggle, I feel, just to stay on my feet. There is no sign of seagulls. All living things might have been swept away, except for a few humans, whose force of will has kept them here. Drying my feet, I put my socks back on. I wrap myself in my big coat, as if the icy assault has already sucked out all my inner heat. I again think of that old Anglo-Saxon poem 'The Seafarer' written by a nameless man. Some lines come back to me now:

Fettered by cold
were my feet,

bound by frost
in cold clasps
where then cares seethed
hot about my heart
a hunger tears from within
the sea-weary soul.
This the man does not know
for whom on land
it turns out most favourably.
How I, wretched and sorrowful,
on the ice-cold sea
dwelt for a winter
in the paths of exile . . .

Shivering under the lukewarm sun, I walk to a cafe and order a hot drink. Warming myself, I look out of the window, that last line 'in the paths of exile' in my mind. My eyes are following some withered leaves as they are blown across the pavement, when my gaze falls upon a flag outside the cafe. A yellow bar and a blue bar, one above the other, the Ukrainian flag. It too is blown in the wind. Refugees are scattered and blown by the winds of war even to this place, Hastings. And today Hastings is a bleak place, it feels like the edge of the world. Still, there is solidarity here. The winds of history have long scattered people abroad. The Haestingas were blown to this place by northern winds from the third century, and then the Anglo-Saxons, and later the Norman storm ravaged the coast. It never ceases. Just like James Joyce said, history is a nightmare from which there is no awakening. We are in troubled Europe, and Hastings is Europe in spite of Brexit.

Night Tide

Today I have not seen the low tide. The water must have been receding at some point this morning, but I missed it. Finally, when the sun is down, as I look out from my window, I notice the low tide. The sandy part of the beach appears, stretching out softly into the water. No more hard shingles. All smooth and flat. It is almost dark. I must go out to walk on the soft sand.

The beach at low tide is gentle and unreal. A vast sand dune with immense moisture. I walk into the water as far as I can. I have no fear of getting wet as I wear my calf-length rubber boots. Now it is dark. The moon is hidden by clouds. I can make out the shape of the skyline where it separates the water and the sky. I see a few shadows moving about in the distance. I walk towards them, guessing they might be the 'hobby' fishermen – the amateur ones who love the night outing on the sea.

Indeed, three locals in their fifties stand around in front of three long fishing rods. The rods are supported by purposely made tall tripods. On top of each rod, a red light is on. Occasionally a red light blinks. When the red light continues to blink, one of the men runs to the dark wavy distance and pulls the fishing line from the sea. Curious, I stand on the wet sand, watching. The fishing line seems to be incredibly long, stretching into the sea. As the man in the water checks his prey, the other two are drinking something from their cups. Tea or mulled wine? It is too early in the season for mulled wine, but I wonder if tea is sufficient to protect them from the cold. The temperature now, I presume, is around 3 or 5 degrees maximum.

The man comes back from the dark distance, holding a small fish. I walk to him and ask him what he has got.

A dogfish, he tells me. Not a great size. But I'll get some good ones later, he adds, with a loud and manly voice. He doesn't have a strong accent. It is more a generic English one to me, from the southern part of England.

I often get whiting and seabass, the kind of fish that live in the shallow water, he says. They prefer to stay in mixed sea and sand bed.

How long will you stay on the beach? I ask.

A few more hours, probably until one in the morning.

One in the morning. Is that the time the tide will change? I wonder to myself. I am amazed that he doesn't feel the night bite at all. Whereas I cannot feel my fingers and toes any more. On the way back from the beach, I try to remember the last time I ate a dogfish. It must have been a very long time ago. Perhaps not in England, or Europe. It must have been in China, in my home province. I remember the shape, long, thin, like a sea eel, but with small fins. It tasted rubbery, like a poor man's dish, at least that was how my family thought. The rich people would eat smooth dishes, not fried dogfish, for supper.

Suddenly, in the quiet darkness, I hear the sound of an explosion. I turn and look around. What was that? Then, moments later, a few more explosions. The sky behind the hills is illuminated by hues of red momentarily. Then all dark and silent again. War? I wonder with an electric stab of fear. Or am I hallucinating? The tide is still receding. I walk towards the sea bank. Gradually, I hear more sounds. Well, I think I am hearing all this: the distant sirens, the rumble of some deep transmission of force. The earth shakes slightly. Unable to move, I freeze on the beach, listening. Then a few moments later, I hear the crunch of feet on the shingles, the grind of boats twisted by the tide and torrent of the swell, the clamour of men's voices crying '*allez*'. Yes, I think I hear some kind of French being spoken. The dim movement of a host of men and horses. The moon is still hidden by a cloud, but it is gradually coming out. The rumble comes again. Should I run? But run to where? A lightning flash, then a plume arises where the sea bank is. I hear more speaking. Men's rough and coarse voices. This time I make out it is Russian. Shielding my head, I hurl myself on the wet sand.

Time passes. There is no one on the beach now. The fishermen have long gone and I am alone on the shingle bed. I sit up, looking around. But there is nobody there, only the waves moving gently. I see a tiny light in the distance out at sea, perhaps a fishing boat? The buildings by the bank are illuminated under the street lamps. Rows of houses stand solemnly aligned, each window is lit up with warm light. I can even see some fairy lights twinkling. It is late. I must get back home. I am tired. I will plunge into my bed. I will sleep. Just like all other people in Hastings, all the Haestingas, ancient and modern, all fall asleep after a day's work and thoughts. I will wake up, the dawn light will enter my curtainless flat, I will hear the waves and watch the tides rise. I will go out and see the ocean in the fresh wind, just like all the people here, welcoming another morning by the sea.

Acknowledgements

My editor Kaiya Shang and my agent Rebecca Carter are the two people who contributed most to the laborious work of revision on this book. As always, Clara Farmer and Graeme Hall have stood firmly by my projects, a heartfelt thank you!

I also benefited greatly from the research of the wonderful historian Marc Morris and especially his work *The Anglo-Saxons: A History of the Beginnings of England* and *The Norman Conquest*. During my research, I loved reading the local paper, the *Hastings Independent*, a constant source of anecdotes and information. The quotes I have used from *Anglo-Saxon Chronicle* are mainly from the online source of Project Gutenberg, www.gutenberg.org, a version translated by J. A. Giles, as well as a version edited by Bob Carruthers and published by Pen & Sword, 2013. Needless to say, whatever errors remain in my text are solely my own.

I am extremely grateful for the support of the following people: Hugh Stewart (for your early reading and notes), Katherine Fry (for many years of your excellent copy edits), Loren Wolfe, Gareth Evans, Andrew Kotting, Anne Witchard, Paul French, Anne Rademacher, Iain Sinclair, Kate Griffin, Philipe Ciompi, Victoria Murray-Browne, Asia Choudhry, Rosanna Hildyard, Polly Dorner, Jessie Spivey, Stephen Parker, Eoin Dunne, Becca Thorne, and the whole Chatto and Vintage team.

And of course, my eternal gratitude to Steve and Moon, along with her witty thoughts.

List of Artworks

All photos are by the author unless otherwise noted